HIGHER EDUCATION
IN THE INFORMATION AGE

HIGHER EDUCATION
IN THE INFORMATION AGE

Edited by
Everette E. Dennis
Craig L. LaMay

Transaction Publishers
New Brunswick (U.S.A.) and London (U.K.)

Second printing 1994

Copyright © 1993 by Transaction Publishers, New Brunswick, New Jersey 08903. Originally published as a special double issue of the *Gannett Center Journal*, Spring-Summer 1991, Copyright © by The Freedom Forum Media Studies Center and The Freedom Forum.

Library of Congress Catalog Number: 92-28069
ISBN: 1-56000-651-X
Printed in the United States of America

        Library of Congress Cataloging-in-Publication Data
Higher education in the information age / edited by Everette E. Dennis, Craig L. LaMay.

    p. cm.—
    ISBN 1-56000-651-X
    1. Public relations—Universities and colleges—United States. 2. Education, Higher—Social aspects—United States. I. Dennis, Everette E. II. LaMay, Craig L.
LB2342.8.H54   1992
659.2'937873—dc20

                                    92-28069
                                       CIP

Contents

"In the more than 20 years that I have worked at the crossroads of universities and the media," writes Duke University's senior vice president for public affairs, "I have seen a steady deterioration in the confidence and belief in the integrity each brings to its assessment of the other's work. . . . The academy doesn't understand how the press operates, . . . and there is ample evidence that the press is remarkably ignorant of the major issues facing higher education." To make things worse, universities and the media both suffer from the debilitating institutional arrogance. What does the future hold?

Part I   The Information Factory

"The university as a repository of social knowledge that is preserved and developed in the public interest may be rapidly disappearing," write the authors, social scientists from Canada's York University. "In its place a new institutional form is emerging, distinguished by its ability to define its markets, cultivate entrepreneurial professors, attract corporate clients and secure intellectual property rights."

In a world where universities pitch education as a product rather than a turn of mind, it's not surprising that *U.S. News & World Report*'s annual "Best American Colleges" issue should be such a celebrated—and dreaded—event. But what does the *U.S. News* survey really tell us about higher education in America? Not much, says a teacher, and "as though to the healing waters," he guides the reader to the expert counsel of another age.

"The lifeblood of a university, particularly a private one, is favorable publicity," writes the president emeritus of Carnegie Mellon. But there is a downside to the publicity machine as well, he cautions, and he recounts his own experiences with the media as he examines his belief that "universities should not be viewed like any other institution subject to investigative journalism."

"Although national journalists may go to a broad range of institutions for backgrounders, they almost invariably turn to experts from a few select institutions to appear on camera or for colorful quotes," writes a journalism educator. In the expert game, he charges, a scholar's university affiliation is more important to the media than expertise itself, or even ideology, a system that would have intrigued C. Wright Mills.

"After giving more than 100 news media interviews between August 2 and the end of the gulf war," writes a well-known Middle East scholar, his efforts came to "about three minutes of airtime and two column inches of quoted opinion." Looking at the war's chaotic aftermath, which he argues might well have been averted, the author evaluates the media's behavior and offers advice to other scholars on how to approach life as a soundbite.

In the competition for students, resources and faculty, universities are discovering the op-ed page as a vehicle for national and regional visibility. But the marriage between academia and journalism is a bumpy one, and occurs largely through the efforts of intermediaries. The director of editorial services at Washington University, one of the first schools to begin an op-ed placement program, discusses the hard work that got it started and the soft touch that keeps it going.

Sure college sports are corrupt, but they help pay for educational programs. Not so, says an authority on college sports financing: Most university athletic programs lose money, lots of it, then rob educational coffers to balance their books. Surprised? Most sports editors and reporters would be too. "With few exceptions," the author says, "most are badly informed about the educational operations and missions of the schools whose teams they cover."

Part II   Journalism in the University

Are university magazines really journalism—or just puff for the alumni? That depends on each magazine's editor and the administration's willingness to withstand inside examination, says the founding editor of *Columbia* magazine. Most magazines are on short chokes, she says, but a handful of others—from public and private universities around the country—offer some of the best journalistic coverage of higher education to be found anywhere.

"In a market where editors balance daily deadlines with term papers and exams, writers are either underpaid or not paid at all, and papers are often funded by the very administrations they're trying to 'watchdog,' it's not easy to produce a consistently solid news product," writes the author, an editor at *U. The National College Newspaper*. From big-budget papers to shoestring affairs, she selects 15 of the nation's best campus dailies.

"Being at the margins of two prominent and powerful social institutions—the press and the university—seems to describe the position of journalism education," writes the author, himself a journalism educator. Unfortunately, he says, such professional marginality has been the cause of perennial career anxiety rather than celebrated as a "fortunate expatriation," an opportunity for a unique monitoring role.

Part III   Wired Campuses

In 1983 Brown University launched an ambitious project to electronically extend the reach of researchers there far beyond the campus confines, an effort that became a model for similar projects elsewhere. Here Brown's librarian recounts the building of the University's network and argues for the role of information specialists in shaping NREN, the proposed national research network.

"While the debate about the tension between teaching and research rages, some technologically proficient scholars are quietly utilizing technology to introduce active scholarship into the undergraduate curriculum," writes the author, a mathematician. But these tools may wither on the vine if the information and education "industries" can't find room for collaboration, and the nation the will to invest in its schools, colleges and universities.

Part IV   Free Expression on Campus

"Education has always inspired fear among those who want to keep the existing distributions of power and wealth as they are," writes the author, a respected political scientist. "Some of us radicals have somehow managed to get tenure, but far from dominating higher education, we remain a carefully watched minority."

"Higher education in this country has been transformed into a species of ideological indoctrination," argues a well-known critic of the academy. "What we are facing is nothing less than a challenge to the fundamental premises that have traditionally supported both liberal education and a liberal democratic polity."

Part V   Book Review

Earlier in this century the most vigorous criticism of higher education came from the political left. Today almost all of it comes from the right, as the five books in this review attest. All five, says the author, one of journalism education's most respected leaders, "raise issues that are fateful for higher education and point to serious problems on campus," but only one is written in the spirit of open dialogue. "The conclusion is inescapable that the existing partners in this debate, with some notable exceptions, have given up all hope for democracy and education however much they invoke both."

Preface

In April 1991, as spring semester drew to a close, students at the City University of New York (CUNY) took over class and administration buildings at 12 of the system's 21 campuses, eventually shutting down six of them. They were protesting a proposed $500 annual tuition increase that, combined with an earlier $200 increase and deep cuts in the state's Tuition Assistance Program, would effectively raise student tuitions more than 60 percent. Eventually other students, fearful of not graduating or losing the semester, took the campuses back; when the state legislature in Albany finally voted on its budget that summer, the tuition increase was less than $500 — but there was an increase.

For nearly 100 years — until 1976 — CUNY was free, open to anyone who could gain admission. It has long been a symbol of hope and opportunity to working-class and immigrant students who otherwise could not afford to attend college, and includes among its distinguished graduates Jonas Salk, Irving Howe, Colin Powell, Gertrude Elion and many others — among them 11 Nobel laureates.

A college education, far more than a primary and secondary one, has long been a material luxury in American life, to say nothing of an intellectual one. Fewer than 38 percent of Americans have ever attended college at all, and only about half that number hold bachelor's degrees. The GI Bill-driven boom that filled the nation's burgeoning state universities with young (mostly) white men after World War II greatly democratized American higher education, but the system has never been a public stewardship. Today many universities are increasingly devoted to private-sector research rather than public learning, to productivity rather than democratic discourse, and, because of greatly diminished financing opportunities from the federal and state governments, have grown increasingly exclusive of poor, working- and lower-middle-class students, many of them people of color. Economist Robert Reich, among many others, has called this growing disparity of educational opportunity one of the critical social issues of the next generation.

At the same time, as proponents of the American system of higher education point out, it is the most open and egalitarian in the world, if not also the "best." Charging that the issue of escalating tuitions has been greatly exaggerated by the media, former Harvard President Derek Bok told the American Society of Newspaper Editors in 1991 that 80 percent of Americans attending college pay less than $2,500 a year, the full cost of their tuitions having been subsidized through financial aid and work-study programs. The nation's many public and private universities include a preponderant number of the world's most revered centers of learning and research — as well as colleges whose legal responsibility, if not their bureaucratic imperative, is to accept virtually any student with a pulse and the wherewithal to pay. Taken as a whole, higher education is perhaps the only American institution that enjoys a positive balance of trade: Many more foreign students come to study at American universities than do Americans go to study abroad.

At one level, of course, casting higher education in purely economic terms runs contrary to the belief of those who have experienced it that "higher" should mean intellectually liberating, not merely materially advantageous. But for a substantial number of students and their families the "liberation" of higher education is economic opportunity; higher education has always been a crucible of class and social position, particularly in other Western democracies, and the more accessible American system is almost by design, if not default, a vehicle for social mobility. When Congress passed the GI Bill in 1944, for example, allowing thousands of returning servicemen to attend college, its intent was less to advance the intellectual life of the nation than to avoid a return to the massive unemployment of the 1930s. In all, more than 7.8 million veterans of World War II took advantage of the GI Bill's educational provisions.

To a lesser — and less understood — extent, Americans also trumpet the university's role in fostering intellectual liberty, but invariably that too gets boiled down to economic issues, or at least political ones, as factions within and without the university squabble over the allocation and application of limited resources, and as universities compete for faculty and students. Today, for example, when many of the nation's finest universities are struggling with budget cuts, the intellectual core of the academy is the object of the most fierce political wrangling in almost half a century.

In such a system it is entirely reasonable that one of the most anticipated and ballyhooed media events in higher education is the annual *U.S. News & World Report* ranking of American colleges. A quick "consumer's guide" to the educational marketplace, the ranking is the object of scorn and derision from university presidents, public affairs officers, faculty and others, many of whom decry the annual rite as symbolic of the poor media coverage given higher education.

At the same time administrators recognize the ranking's impact — one university president noted that applications for admission increased 30 percent after *U.S. News* ranked his school among its best — and they are themselves preoccupied with marketing their "products" and communicating through the media to the public. Not coincidentally, Heidrick & Struggles, one of the premier head-hunting firms that specialize in finding university presidents, ranks fundraising and public relations skills first and second respectively among the qualifications most important on prospective candidates' resumes.

The university's success over the years in promoting a positive public image of itself has been astounding. For years Americans have ranked colleges and universities, their administrators and faculty, among those institutions and professionals for whom they have the most respect. As Ernest Boyer has pointed out, universities are the only social institutions in America for which Americans will put bumper stickers on their cars and pennants in their bedrooms, willingly and without embarrassment, whether their alma mater is Harvard or the most humble community college. Similarly, though perhaps more ominously, the "boosters" and fans who flock by the hundreds of thousands to college sports events are for the most part uninvolved in the academic life of the universities whose teams they support.

In the 1980s all that began to change, a transformation probably precipitated by Education Secretary William Bennett's bashing at the gates of academe. One reporter, responsible for covering three leading research universities within a 25-mile radius, told us that while she personally distrusted Bennett's educational agenda, his attack on the education establishment's traditional prerogatives effectively transformed her beat from a passive to an active one. Rather than obediently rewriting university press releases, she said, she was suddenly expected to ask questions about university programs and operations — to make a story out of higher education. Shortly afterward, in 1987, Allan Bloom's *The Closing of the American Mind* firmly established the market for media attentive to the "crisis" in higher education.

Today that market is flourishing, not only in trade books but in magazines, newspapers, television. It remains to be seen whether the media will identify this "crisis" or merely enlarge and confuse it. The only thing that seems certain is that there is a deepening disaffection between the nation's colleges and universities and our media system; neither is happy with the other's performance, and neither knows what message to send to the public.

Those inside higher education complain that they are seen narrowly and mainly in terms of conflict, controversy and scandal, and sports. The media, they say, do not attend to the more subtle, systemic issues that are of greatest concern within higher education, nor do they understand its unique institutional character.

For their part, media people say (and many in higher education agree with them) that higher education itself is to blame for much of this deficiency, playing hard to get on critical stories and being unresponsive to media deadlines. Many administrators and scholars are less than adept in communicating with the media, and often project a public image of arrogance or detachment that inspires anything but confidence.

But even as the leaders of the news media say that colleges and universities are important, much of the regular coverage in the field is frighteningly trivial, more akin to alumni notes than news. People looking for regular and intelligent news of higher education can find it only in the *Chronicle of Higher Education* — which is aimed at educators and college administrators — and a few well-written, well-edited university magazines.

The theme of this volume then, is that there is a crisis in higher education, a crisis of *knowledge* — who produces it, controls it, uses it, benefits by it. These issues are central to the character of both the university and the mass media. Indeed, as institutions they may have more in common than they realize. Speaking on the 30th anniversary of his famous "Vast Wasteland" speech, former FCC Chairman and Annenberg Washington Program Director Newton N. Minow reminded his audience that, more than any college or university, "the most important educational institution in America is television. More people learn more each day, each year, each lifetime from television than from any other source." For most people — including those with college degrees — even print media are more important as a lifelong source of information than universities.

Properly understood, the information issues common to both higher education and the media have profound implications for public life. "Properly understood," of course, is the prerequisite for "intelligently discussed"; if the relationship between the media and higher education is to change for the better, each must begin in its own house. The media must see the value in devoting more resources to covering higher education, to understanding its role in the nation's economic affairs and in improving the public's quality of life; in turn, those in higher education must gain a better understanding of the mass media, of how they work and what they do, and they must develop a more sophisticated attitude about the role of publicity on campus.

The curious relationship between these two institutions is the topic of "Mixed (Up) Messages: Universities and the Media," the introductory essay by John F. Burness, Duke University senior vice president for public affairs. "In the more than 20 years that I have worked at the crossroads of universities and the media," Burness writes, "I have seen a steady deterioration in the confidence and belief in the integrity each brings to its assessment of the other's work." The university has the most to lose in this relationship, but it also has the most to gain: "Universities will learn to communicate more effectively and directly to alumni, parents, students, government officials and others." Still at issue is what the larger public — those not already in the social and economic folds that include higher education — will learn about the nation's colleges and universities. If the media continue as they have, Burness warns — and he is not sanguine about the likelihood of their doing better — then the prospects for enlarging higher education's reach and potential are not bright.

The following section of the volume, "The Information Factory," at once broadens and narrows Burness' view of higher education. In "Social Knowledge and Market Knowledge: Universities in the Information Age," Canadian social scientists Howard Buchbinder and Janice Newson argue that the modern university has largely abandoned the higher aspirations of education for the monetary ones of business enterprise. Today, they say, a university's success is measured by the "ability to define its markets, cultivate entrepreneurial professors, attract corporate clients and secure intellectual property rights." Their argument is complemented by Thomas Bergmann's essay "Acquiring an Alma Mater or Achieving an Education," a sharp review of the methods and purposes

of *U.S. News & World Report*'s annual ranking of American colleges —
and a pointed analysis of what higher education has lost.

That the *U.S. News* survey should each year be an occasion for dread
and celebration at universities across the country underscores the media's
role in shaping the education enterprise, the topic of "Gumshoes at the
Gates," by Carnegie Mellon University President Emeritus Richard M.
Cyert. While he acknowledges that the media provide universities with
the lifeblood of publicity, Cyert condemns much of the reporting on
higher education and asks whether universities shouldn't be exempt from
the kind of media scrutiny given other institutions. Following him,
Lawrence Soley of the University of Minnesota, Richard Bulliet of
Columbia and Trudi Spigel of Washington University offer differing
views of the interplay between scholarship and journalism, raising questions about public interest and private and institutional gain. Closing this
section, Indiana University Professor Murray Sperber debunks many of
the most cherished myths about big-time college sports — myths cham-
pioned by academics and journalists alike — arguing that corruption not
only hurts college athletes, but imposes unacceptably high costs on other
students and throttles many educational programs.

Universities have their own media, of course, from alumni magazines
to student broadsheets. In "Grub Street in the Groves of Academe," one
of higher education's best known journalists, Ceil Cleveland, argues that
while many university magazines are fluff for the alumni, a handful of
others offer some of the best writing on higher education to be found
anywhere. Following her, Jacki Hampton, the managing editor of *U. The
National College Newspaper*, offers her list of the 15 best student-run
dailies on America's campuses. Closing out the section on "Journalism
in the University," communications scholar Douglas Birkhead argues
that journalism educators, long marginalized both as academics and
professionals, should celebrate their "fortunate expatriation" and explore
the opportunities it offers to monitor the profession.

In "Wired Campuses," a section on information technology's transforming potential in the university, a librarian and a mathematician look
at the future of electronic research and interactive teaching technologies.
Brown University Librarian Merrily Taylor recounts Brown's prototype
efforts to "network" scholars and researchers in "The World at Our
Fingertips," and argues for a prominent role for information specialists
in shaping the proposed National Research and Education Network

(NREN). In "The Silicon Scholar," William Graves, director of the Institute for Academic Technology at the University of North Carolina, explores the multimedia manipulation of research to benefit teaching, and asks if the information and education "industries," state and federal governments, will effectively develop them.

In a special section on "Free Expression on Campus," Boston University political scientist Howard Zinn and *New Criterion* Editor Roger Kimball offer opposing responses to the simple question we put to them: "Is higher education the leading institutional champion of free expression in America?"

Finally, communications scholar James W. Carey examines five books on "The Academy and its Discontents," all written from the political right. All the books "raise issues that are fateful for higher education and point to serious problems on campus," Carey says, but only one is written in the spirit of open dialogue. "Any substantial change in education is going to require a new coalition of people drawn from across the political spectrum who revolt against the uncivil lines and habits of argument that are at the moment destroying the possibilities of public life and with them the people . . . who would benefit most from a less ideological, more pragmatic and generally more civil form of discourse."

THE EDITORS

Introduction
Higher Education in the Information Age

In the modern era, higher education in America has rarely been far from public consciousness. Closely associated with upward mobility, the university has something of a love-hate relationship with the larger society. Universities are at once prestigious and at the same time scorned for being elitist and out of touch. Parents sacrifice mightily for their children's college education while balking at support for higher education's growing needs. While the university is probably society's most admired and respected institution, it is also the subject of harsh criticism from conservative forces unhappy with change on the campus, and the target of reformist critics who are dissatisfied with the lack of change. Thus, the university is is under seige on many fronts. There is, of course, a question about how a venerable institution which had its origins in 13th-century Bologna is to remain fresh and relevant in what is now commonly called "the information society." This term was used at first to describe an anticipated moment in time when more people would be employed in manipulating symbols — that is acquiring, processing and disseminating information —than in industry and agriculture. The term has recently taken on a larger meaning, according to the British commentator Anthony Smith — that indeed a culture of information has now emerged, best symbolized by the computer — that is a social force in and of itself, and a threat even to national boundaries. The dilemma of higher education to connect with and help shape the information society is the subject of this book. Closely connected to that concern is higher education's relationship with a central force in the information society, that of the mass media. Three interrelated features of that relationship are explored in this volume:

- higher education as a communicator, both through the news media and by other means to the larger society;

- the role of the media as educator, that of taking up where formal education leaves off in keeping people informed about the society around them, and finally;

- higher education as a subject of media content, whether in the news, opinion or entertainment media.

1

Together these three different but closely connected functions define the present status and probable future of higher education in the information age. As a communicator, higher education wants desperately to be understood, appreciated and supported by the public and various constituency groups ranging from scholars and professionals in various fields, to other institutions like business or science, not to mention such key publics as students, faculty, alumni and parents. To this end higher education has developed a public communication aparatus with information and public affairs offices, news bureaus, special events and so on. In a somewhat more subtle fashion, higher education also operates public radio and television stations, and publishes magazines and newsletters. University presidents are typically the chief communicators, assisted by administrative officers with specific operational and technical assignments. In a more general sense, the university also communicates through its students, faculty, alumni, parents of students and sports establishment. Through its teaching, research and service activities, the university further connects itself with the larger society. Every university therefore has a personality that is a product of its character, traditions, and curricular offerings that give it an identity, in particular an identity that distinguishes it from its peers. There is a parting of the ways for most students and graduates from their formal education. Even though educators have promoted lifelong learning for decades, most educated Americans do not return to the classroom or even engage in continuing education once they leave the campus. These are among our liveliest and best informed people, yet without continuing formal learning in a rapidly changing society, how can they continue to benefit from advances in knowledge, whether in their specific field or in education generally? The answer, like it or not, is by paying attention to the media, which are the central nervous system of the culture, and the source for new and updated information across virtually all fields of interest. Thus, while neither the news or entertainment media promise to systematically keep track of everything that education is concerned with, they do in a fashion cover public life and attendant institutional fields, ranging from the arts to the military and many others. Years ago, Henry Luce gave *Time* magazine a list of "departments" that virtually cover the waterfront in a fashion that latter day computer experts called a "menu" of topics and subjects, and that broad-ranging mission has been picked up by different media ranging from scholarly journals to supermarket tabloids. All purport to cover society, albeit with different degrees of sophistication and with different intensity levels. For better or worse, it is in these realms that many of the great debates of our society are played out. For the news media, higher education is also a "beat" or a subject of interest to be covered as news or exploited as entertainment. There are education editors and reporters in major media and specialized magazines, journals, databases, newsletters and other media covering education. How well do the media cover the education "beat"? Not very, say the critics, who complain that higher education is a misunderstood institution and blame the media for that condition. Still, the great educational reform movements, the debates over multiculturalism and political correctness and other campus issues do get news ink and television news time. Or they are woven into screenplays and television scripts. The economic dilemma of higher education, the foibles of university presidents, campus unrest and scandals, racism and research also regularly make news as does the mighty college sports establishment. Without much doubt, the coverage of higher education is not the media's top priority and neither is it done with any great distinction; still, it is on the agenda and apparently getting better. Whether that minor improvement is adequate or not invariably raises even more debate. However, most media people we know readily admit that they do not cover the field adequately and blame lack of reader/viewer interest and barriers to information erected by college officials for the problem. Universities respond that they do not get fair or adequate treatment, and that the news is all too often sensational and superficial. So it is an imperfect world. But in the manner of educational reform commissions it is not difficult for thoughtful people to dissect the media-higher education dilemma and find at least partial solutions to the problems. That two institutions both caught up in an information society depend on each other is clearly irrefutable. This volume attempts to further define and detail the debate and to assess the role, purpose and consequences of the information society for higher education. Along the way, the mass media play a starring, if not always critically acclaimed role. In the end, it is hoped that such discourse will stimulate public debate and foster public understanding. To that end this book is dedicated.

This book is a revised and edited version of "Higher Education in the Information Age," which was the Spring-Summer 1991 issue of the *Gannett Center Journal*. Subsequently, the Journal changed its name to the *Media Studies Journal*, reflecting the new name of its parent organization, the Freedom Forum Media Studies Center of Columbia University, formerly the Gannett Center for Media Studies. The Center is an operating program of The Freedom Forum of Arlington, Va., a foundation devoted to freedom of expression, especially free press and speech. The Freedom Forum was formerly known as the Gannett Foundation.

1

Mixed (Up) Messages: Universities and the Media

John F. Burness

Following a speech on the Duke University campus, George Will, the noted chronicler of our national pastime and other issues, was asked the following question: "If you were on a small island in the middle of the ocean and could have either Sam Donaldson or Phil Donahue for company, whom would you choose?" Without missing a beat Will said, "I'd start swimming."

A reasonable response. But unlike Will, who can always turn a question in the direction he chooses as he crafts his columns, universities and the press can't seem to avoid each other these days. More to the point, in the more than 20 years that I have worked at the intersection of universities and the media, I have seen a steady deterioration in the confidence and belief in the integrity each brings to its assessment of the other's work, with potentially serious implications both for America's universities and for American society. There's more than enough blame to go around in assessing why this relationship has sunk to such a low point. In this article I hope to place the issues and challenges facing the relationship in some perspective.

The press and academia have a great deal in common. Each has a tradition of expanding knowledge and educating the public to be enlightened and involved citizens in a democratic society. Each enjoys a remarkable freedom from state interference relative to its counterparts in other countries. The United States is one of the few (if not the only) nations in the world which doesn't have a cabinet-level office for a minister of information. Scholars in the United States enjoy a degree of

5

academic freedom — the ability to pursue research and teach in ways they deem appropriate to their topics without outside interference — to a degree that is envied by scholars around the world.

Neither the press nor higher education in America is monolithic, yet each is often seen as such. The very diversity of the media in America — weekly and daily newspapers, tabloids, weekly and monthly magazines, television, radio and trade publications — is one of its greatest strengths. The *New York Times* and the check-out counter tabloids are as different from each other (notwithstanding the *Times'* printing the name of the accuser in the Palm Beach rape allegation) as Neiman Marcus is to K-mart, yet to the public the media are one large undifferentiated whole — "the press." The same can be said for higher education, which in the United States consists of private and public institutions, graduate research universities and institutes, undergraduate liberal arts colleges, two-year colleges, religiously affiliated institutions and trade schools. To think of Duke and the schools which advertise their services on matchbook covers as being even remotely the same defies the imagination. Yet, as often as not in my experience, the public and many in the press see higher education as one coherent industry.

Each also has the unfortunate tendency when challenged to be instantly defensive and to assume that those who challenge don't (but should) understand how it works. Also, too often each assumes that any criticism is a fundamental challenge, either to the press' First Amendment protection or to the academy's academic freedom protection. It is this perceived arrogance that probably does as much to harm public perception of both the press and higher education as any other characteristic.

Simply put, the academy doesn't understand how the press operates, what its priorities are, what constitutes a story worthy of press attention, what being "on deadline" means, etc. The academy resents the press's inability to "understand," its apparent preference for images over ideas and issues, and its reliance on "soundbites" to explain complex issues.

In fairness, there is ample evidence that the press is remarkably ignorant of the major issues facing higher education, yet it thinks it understands them. In 1987 I commissioned a study by the national survey research firm Yankelovich, Skelly and White/Clancy, Shulman, Inc. (the survey firm used by *Time* magazine) to assess the views of opinion leaders about higher education, and particularly the research universities. The opinion leaders surveyed were from the federal government, the major corporations, and the media, and the survey consisted of 45-minute to one-hour interviews with a total of 235 people, including 43 opinion leaders from major national media — editorial writers, syndicated columnists, magazine editors, broadcast anchors and commentators. The survey was conducted at the height of then-Secretary of Education Bill Bennett's attacks on the quality and the academic and fiscal integrity of higher education; it concluded that of the three groups of opinion leaders, the press was by far "the least knowledgeable." For example, when asked to identify the major issues facing American higher education, all of the groups surveyed listed rising costs (tuition) as the leading problem, but only 2 percent of the media listed "need for student aid/need for student financial support" (as compared to 24 percent of the government leaders).

Consistent with that finding, 33 percent of the government officials identified funding of universities (the institutions' financial problems) as critical, while only 9 percent of the press did. The fact is that between 1978 and 1988, the federal government had dropped from providing 47 percent to 17 percent of the total financial aid pool in the form of direct grants to support access by needy and middle-class students to college. By 1988, 80 percent of federal financial aid was in the form of loans — up from 50 percent in 1978. It is debatable whether this transfer of responsibility for assisting needy and middle-class students from the federal government to parents and institutions may be appropriate public policy, but its impact on universities and university finance has been enormous, a fact that Yankelovich's research demonstrated the press did not understand. According to Arthur Hauptman, an economist who specializes in higher education finance, roughly 25 percent of the annual increase in tuition at private universities during the 1980s may be attributable to the institutions' filling the gap left by the federal government's shift from grant funds to loan funds. That 25 percent alone would essentially represent the increase in tuition above inflation during the time period.

That the press failed to appreciate the gravity and implications of the financial aid crisis may not be surprising, since Secretary Bennett had done a masterful job in misrepresenting the issue to the public, with the press performing as a willing if uninformed ally. Bennett had argued that universities raised tuition so rapidly because they had a third-party payer (the government) that ultimately would pay the bills. The universities, quite unaccustomed to histrionic political attacks of this type, went into a defensive posture and, instead of explaining the facts and making their case, criticized Bennett for the presumptiveness of the attack itself. The result was predictable.

On another of the Yankelovich questions the press was also remarkably uninformed. When asked whether the amount of money the federal government allocates to universities for maintenance and upgrading of research facilities and equipment over the previous 10 years had increased or decreased, 56 percent responded that it had increased or stayed the same. According to the National Science Foundation, in 1968 the federal government provided $2.1 billion in support of facilities at America's colleges and universities; by 1988 the figure had dropped to about $400 million. When inflation is considered, in 1988 the government was providing less than 5 percent as much money to support facilities at colleges and universities as it had 20 years earlier. Anyone who understands the impact of changes in technology on laboratories and instrumentation or who appreciates the life cycle of an educational facility should be able to understand the impact of this shift in federal policy on the infrastructure costs of higher education.

One result — in the absence of previous federal programs that relied on merit review — has been the emergence of hundreds of millions of dollars in congressional pork barrel funding for higher education facilities. Another is increasing tuitions, as private universities have had to rebuild their physical plant to meet contemporary instructional and research needs. And finally, since some depreciation of facilities in which federally funded research occurs can be billed to the government, it has contributed greatly to the increase in the indirect cost rates that are now under intense congressional scrutiny.

Higher education has made efforts repeatedly to educate the public about this issue, but without notable success. A 1988 White House Science Council committee, chaired by industrialist David Packard and present Presidential Science Adviser Allen Bromley, estimated that the facilities backlog at America's colleges and universities approached $15 billion. But there was little flash (no man bites dog) and very little coverage of the issue. That continues to be the case.

I've seen little evidence in the past few years that would lead me to think that higher education can realistically expect much better reporting. Popular newsmagazines have reduced by 10 to 15 lines the amount of per-page copy so they can provide better graphics. Major newspapers such as the *New York Times* have set limits — 1,500 words I'm told by a former education reporter at the *Times* — on the length of a higher education story editors will generally accept. And as the same *Times* reporter told me, most of the serious stories about higher education that he knows about are sufficiently complex that 1,500 words will barely make a dent in the context in which they must be told. Given the crisis in the nation's primary and secondary schools in America, the serious problems of higher education are naturally on a back burner. The result, as one thoughtful reporter from a national paper told me, is that higher education "shouldn't look for any help from the press in telling its story."

Nowhere has this been more dramatically borne out than by the recent spate of reporting about "political correctness" at Duke. It is painful to me, after more than 20 years of working closely with reporters, to see how superficial the reporting on this issue has been, when in fact the issues that underlie it are critical to American society. Debates over the canon have been portrayed as death struggles between Western civilization and contemporary approaches to literature, when in fact both thrive. The utterances of individual faculty are reported as statements of institutional policy. The minds of students are reputed to be threatened but, with the rarest of exceptions, no reporter has actually interviewed students here. Claims of mind control or thought police in the classroom are taken at face value. Yet when a *Washington Post* reporter actually took the time to sit in on a group of classes taught by the so-called radicals, her conclusion was that

- ... if the proof of the pudding is the pedagogy, Duke should be blessing its stars and superstars. During a month of eclectic attendance at courses in the English department, I was consistently impressed by the quality of the teaching. My own graduate studies ended in the late 60s, just about the time that the deconstructionist theories of Jacques Derrida were starting to make waves in American critical circles. The theoretical approaches in some classes . . . were therefore new to me. But what was both familiar and admirable was the spectacle of good teachers interacting with bright, well-prepared students, students who gave every indication of feeling free to speak their minds.

- In English 168 ("Afro-American Literature"), . . . there was no political agenda in sight.

- In English 329, a graduate seminar, Stanley Fish took on Milton's *Areopagitica*. Though the new theorists are often portrayed as rejecting the canon, Fish's specialty is the ultra-canonical Milton. . . . In Fish's rigorous rhetorical analysis, *Areopagitica*, traditionally regarded as a classic defense of a free press, became "a self-consuming artifact, . . . a work which in a variety of ways invalidates

itself." Not only did Fish demonstrate that Milton's devotion to free speech and
a free press was severely limited, he also argued that Milton's view of truth had
a good deal in common with the deconstructionists'. For Milton, imperfect man
can only grasp at pieces of Truth; knowledge of the whole is deferred until
Christ's Second Coming. For the deconstructionists, Fish noted, knowledge of
the truth is also deferred. Eternally.

It was a bravura performance.

Of the more than 50 reporters from around the country and from within
easy distance of Duke that I've spoken with in the past six months about
the "radical" Duke English department, the *Post* reporter is the only one
who actually could report on what is happening in the classroom from
first-hand experience.

I don't mean to imply that third- or second-hand sources are not useful
ways to establish background for a story, but the soundbite approach to
this issue employed by the great majority of reporters who have written
about Duke does little to inspire confidence in the accuracy of the
reporting. I would be the first to acknowledge that some members of the
Duke faculty have said seemingly outlandish things in the course of the
debates about deconstructionism and "political correctness," reminding
me that there is nothing inherent in academic freedom that protects
anyone who wishes to make a fool of himself from doing so. But at a
time when words such as "politically correct," "diversity," "multiculturalism," "liberal" and "conservative" have different meanings to
different people, the press's infatuation with the terms has brought more
heat than light to the issues about which they have reported. No one, least
of all the public, has been served by such reporting.

I have been harsh up to now on the press. I am even more critical of
the universities.

In many ways our leading universities are defined by their scientific
research contributions. Public understanding of science and technology
in this country is ambivalent at best. While at Cornell I commissioned a
great deal of research on what people know and understand about
research universities, and the results were both disappointing and edify-
ing. The American research university is a relatively recent phenomenon
(post-World War II and arguably post-Sputnik), and most of its graduates
are now in a position to remember universities *as they were* and don't
understand them as they are today. In my view, the problem is less a
function of the "surface perceptions drawn from the media," as one

university leader has suggested, than it is the failure of those of us who work in research universities to invest the time to educate our many publics about what we do and why what we do is important.

In a wide array of public forums I have been as harshly critical of the press's coverage of the major issues affecting higher education, and in particular the research universities, as perhaps anyone. But I think a case can be made that in the past decade or so the press has made a major effort to improve its coverage of science. The emergence of large and regular sections devoted to science in newspapers and magazines, even increased attention on television, is one manifestation of that. While education sections in newspapers flounder and can't draw advertising, the science sections of the major papers are expanding regularly. Science writing has become a growth industry, notwithstanding the recent downturn in the economy which has led some papers to cut back their science coverage.

During the past few years I have been on separate panels with reporters Ivars Peterson of *Science News* and Walter Sullivan of the *New York Times*. At each of those discussions the question was raised as to whether the cold fusion debacle helped or hindered public understanding of science. Virtually all of the scientists and research administrators in the audience believed that it had been harmful and had led to public distrust of science. The journalists, however, had a quite different view — and, I must confess, I side with them. Their view is that the research process is so little understood by the public that the cold fusion debate did an enormous amount to help an uninformed public understand how the scientific and research processes work, and showed how the self-regulating mechanism of replicating experiments ensures the integrity of the process.

Some in higher education have criticized the popular press for releasing scientific results as a perversion of the peer review process, a process which ensures that the results of research are scrutinized with enormous care prior to publication. In my view that criticism is misplaced. At a time of relatively decreasing funding for research, it is members of the scientific community — rushing to be the first to announce their discoveries in hopes that doing so will secure their position with funding agencies or with patent offices — who should be criticized for premature release of non-peer-reviewed pieces, not the press who report it.

Even the present high-profile discussions of indirect costs — dollars institutions are entitled to bill the government for monies the universities spend to provide an infrastructure to support individual research projects — are widely misunderstood by the academic community. Congressional interest in fraud and misconduct in research — to which the indirect cost discussion is related — is, in my view, a function of two issues. The first is the increased visibility and cost of big science projects such as the supercollider, the human genome, the space program, etc., which naturally led to increased scrutiny, especially by those who would capitalize for political purposes. The second is a more basic issue relating to heightened congressional concern about protecting whistle blowers in an era when the defense department and other federal agencies — as well as the industries that work with them — have dismissed legitimate charges and allegations brought to their attention with occasional catastrophic results, such as the space shuttle disaster or overpayments for defense technology. The general concern for whistle blowers has gradually engulfed virtually all of the agencies and, in my view, is a considerably more important factor in the search for error at the National Institutes of Health, the National Science Foundation or the other agencies that fund research than is any enmity towards science, research or even universities.

Congressional concern, of course, has been compounded by the failure until recently of the agencies, and in some cases the institutions, to put in place policies and procedures that ensure adequate reviews of allegations of misconduct. I know from two different cases with which I have some familiarity that until fairly recently neither the institution involved nor the National Institutes of Health had policies and procedures in place that could withstand the kind of allegations that ultimately emerged, e.g., that the reviews were superficial and that the allegations were not investigated with appropriate diligence. I think the universities are putting such procedures in place, and I hope the federal agencies are as well, but I don't think that could have been said five years ago. And even in the two instances I know something about, when the institution was challenged five years ago it defended policies and procedures that ultimately were proven to be quite inadequate. I don't wish to imply that investigating allegations of misconduct is not a complex issue that requires protecting the rights of both the accused and the accuser. Nor do I wish to imply that there is no great need for clarifying the conflicting array of federal policies and practices that provide less than adequate guidance for researchers and institutions in conflict-of-interest issues. But I do believe that the academic community has contributed to the present situation by not taking it as seriously as we could have and should have. And as a result, public confidence in the integrity of universities and of research has seriously declined.

Moreover the fact that these issues have been used by some in Congress for apparent political gain should not allow the fundamental concerns that led to the investigations to be dismissed. Unfortunately, many in the academy have done exactly that, with the unwitting assistance of many members of the press who neither understand the ambiguity in the government's policies — which make some aspects of the present situation almost inevitable — or who fail to perceive the manipulation of information by those seeking to make political points and generate headlines.

A good part of the problem results from the reluctance of people in the academy to recognize that higher education is in a decidedly changed environment. Several years ago I had lunch with Alan Hammond, the nuclear physicist from Yale who was the editor of the now defunct magazine *Science '84, '85, '86*, etc. I asked him what the principal difference was between the world of science and that of journalism. He told me that whenever he returned an article to a scientist to review for accuracy, the scientist (and I suspect people in the academy in general) tried to turn the article into a journal article for fear that any possible overstatement or understatement would be looked at with disdain by one's peers. That was probably understandable, Hammond said, because the scientist is interested in the content of the article while the journalist, he pointed out, is interested in the context. He concluded that the difference between the two is like that between informing and teaching. I found that to be a useful distinction and description of a fundamental problem that permeates the academy — a reluctance to spend time communicating what we do in a way that is helpful to an uninformed and increasingly skeptical public that doesn't understand our jargon. Academics frequently criticize those who do try to play this role — the Sagans and Cousteaus, for example, who probably have done more to improve interest in and understanding of science than most, but whom the scientific community looks down upon as popularizers.

Two incidents occurred during my time as vice president at Cornell that illustrate this problem. A couple of years ago the University's Boyce Thompson Institute applied for Environmental Protection Agency permission to field test a genetically engineered organism — a cabbage borer — at the University's Geneva Experiment Station. The application would be listed in the Federal Register, available for anyone interested to see. Those who pay attention to these things know that the Jeremy Rifkins of the world spend a great deal of time looking through such documents and then play to the fears of the public by issuing inflammatory statements about the effects of anything that resembles genetic engineering. By generating the first story, Rifkin and his colleagues have masterfully framed public discussion of a large number of scientific issues.

In anticipation of that prospect, Cornell's senior science writer wrote a comprehensive article for distribution to the press, and its release was timed to the University's application to the government. The article, in the form of a backgrounder, was designed to anticipate and answer every question that an uninformed or skeptical public might ask. When we presented it to involved members of our faculty for review, a number of them said they did not want any release on this issue because they thought it would draw attention to the experiment and create controversy, a position their dean essentially supported. Using authority I probably didn't have but was quick to acquire, I established a policy-on-the-fly that any time Cornell applies to any government agency for permission to field test a genetically engineered organism it would simultaneously issue a comprehensive public release. The dean ultimately agreed with my position, which was quickly backed by the provost and the president. We issued that release. The end result was comprehensive national coverage of the research, by both television and print media, with nary a whimper from Rifkin. To the degree that he was mentioned in any of the articles it was usually in the last paragraph.

This common sense approach to the issue was seen to be sufficiently rare for universities that it merited a story in *Science* magazine as an example of how to do this kind of thing correctly. Yet it required — I should hasten to point out — a nontenured administrator to overrule a group of tenured faculty who clearly had not thought the issue through with sufficient care to realize that, like it or not, there would be public attention to their research and they had an obligation to explain it.

The second case involved a member of the faculty whose laboratory on three occasions had been identified by the University's nuclear safety people as violating regulations for the handling of radioactive isotopes. The faculty member was not directly involved, but in all such instances — and although the mishandling of the isotopes in this case presented no danger to anyone and, in fact, had been done by graduate students on all three occasions — faculty members are nonetheless responsible for the administration of their laboratories. The professor in question held one of the most distinguished chairs at Cornell; the provost and I agreed that if we did not act in a prudent and responsible way in the face of repeated violations in the laboratory of a senior scientist, we would send the worst possible signal to other faculty and leave the institution vulnerable to appropriate criticisms from external reviewers. The University closed the faculty member's laboratory for two weeks and publicized that fact in its faculty-staff paper. The professor in question was outraged and, not surprisingly, attempted to override the closing of his laboratory and especially the decision to publicize that closing to the campus community. We did not issue a release to the general public, but were prepared to answer any questions should they have come to us. We also worked closely with the faculty member in charge of nuclear safety (a more junior member of the faculty who had acted courageously) to ensure that we were consistent in what we were saying about the manner in which this institution would treat violations of laboratory procedures.

Over the past several years I have become increasingly convinced that universities must do a better job in communicating clearly and thoughtfully to the audiences on whom they ultimately depend for support. The fact that improving how universities and faculty communicate takes people away from their offices, laboratories and classrooms is an inevitable and increasingly important component of what we *all* must do if academia is to retain and enhance the level of support it receives. The need for universities to be aggressive in this arena is made even more important by the recent federal budget negotiations that for the next five years have frozen at inflation levels the budgets of virtually every agency that funds higher education, including the research agencies.

So there is more than enough blame to go around for the deterioration in the relationship between the press and the universities — What does the future hold? I suspect more of the same. Universities and their faculties will gradually realize that the very changed environment in which they operate will necessitate a far greater openness and an investment in sophisticated, honest communication programs to educate various publics as to what they do, how and why they do it, and why it's so important that they succeed. But they will be doing that after much of the damage from athletic scandals, scientific fraud and misconduct, conflict of interest, and revelations about "inappropriate" expenditures of federal research dollars has seriously undercut the relatively high standing universities historically have held in American life. Like it or not, the universities — even private ones — have become the equivalent of public utilities in the eyes of many segments of the public, and the legal niceties and barriers that may have characterized their relationships with these publics in the past are not likely to continue to serve their interest.

The press will continue to report on these and other issues, but with an even higher degree of cynicism than ever given how far the academy has fallen in the eyes of the public. I am not sanguine about the prospect for improved media coverage given the industry's evolution more and more toward *USA Today*-style journalism, "infotainment" and 20-second soundbites.

In the final analysis, the universities will need to recognize the consequences of their own failures to communicate effectively and the inherent limitations of the media in dealing with complex issues that affect the academy. One inevitable result will be that universities will learn to communicate more effectively and *directly* to alumni, parents, students, government officials and others. If at one time universities, especially research universities, could communicate with alumni largely based on fundraisers' belief that appealing to nostalgia would bring in the dollars, they'll need to rethink that dictum.

A survey I commissioned in 1990 by Gordon Black, *USA Today*'s survey research firm, documents that alumni want to believe their institutions are engaged in the fundamental issues facing the society. They want to believe that the universities are ethical. They want to know of the challenges and opportunities facing their alma maters. If the press's traditional need for conflict in a story means that issues like the financial aid and facilities crises noted earlier aren't in the press's judgement worthy of serious and sustained reportage, then the universities will need to invest in educating their publics through direct communication. This will require university administrations to be more open and honest than they've ever had to be in the past, to be more willing than they have been to acknowledge that they have erred. By recognizing the changed reality of the environment in which they exist and on which they depend, universities are likely to receive a more favorable response from a better informed public and greater respect, even grudging recognition, from the press.

John F. Burness is senior vice president for public affairs at Duke University.

PART I

The Information Factory

2

Social Knowledge and Market Knowledge: Universities in the Information Age

Howard Buchbinder and Janice Newson

Through the sophisticated technology of the much heralded "information age," the war in the Persian Gulf has been absorbed into our cultural repertoire even as it invaded the intimacy of our homes. Alternatively referred to as "Iraq: The Movie" and "Iraq: The TV Game Show," it demonstrated public relations management at its best — the ultimate inversion between the "real thing" and its representation. As bombs exploded in Baghdad, Scud missiles rent the skies over Tel Aviv and Patriots shot into the air in response. The images of war were being skillfully and instantaneously interpreted to viewers in the safety of homes far removed from the events themselves. Strategic arms consultants of all types became instant media celebrities. Information gained through the rapid medium of a television interview became the basis for actively participating in deciding the course of the war. Average citizens were invited on telephone call-in shows to offer their advice on how to proceed — whether to continue the bombing or to start a ground war, whether to take out Saddam Hussein or to focus on his elite Republican Army.

Many average citizens enthusiastically rose to the occasion, never once questioning whether they were sufficiently informed to make such crucial decisions. Rarely did anyone acknowledge that, in spite of its instantaneous and apparently spontaneous character, the information available to them only led to a limited number of conclusions. The player-citizen invariably found his or her advice or viewpoint confirmed or refuted, depending on whether it corresponded or not to the choices made by those who executed the war, those who managed and controlled the information that was made available in the first place. Only now, after the military phase of the war appears to be over, questions begin to surface about the coherence between the instant images, the information that was made available, and the decisions that were actually taken.

It is commonplace by now to say that this war was a showcase for the technological wizardry of the arms industry. Yet equally important, it exposed a critical contradiction between information-age technology on the one hand and the role of information in democratic societies on the other. In the words of the German philosopher Martin Heidegger, "while information in-forms, that is, reports, at the same time it forms, that is, it organizes and directs." The war in the gulf has shown us that instantly transmitted images and on-the-spot 30-second reports that are passed off as "information" may in fact do very little to inform us. Nevertheless, they are critical in organizing and directing our responses to what we think is happening.

The integration, at low cost, of rapid computation and the instantaneous transmission of information has been the major technological advance that has facilitated the global information network that brought the war into our living rooms, says Heather Menzies in her book *Fast Forward and Out of Control*. But recently Anthony Smith has argued that it has been the installation of a new economic system within media industries throughout the world that deserves our attention at this time. Because of this system, he says, the ownership of information itself has become the critical concern and the focus of much activity. During the conduct of the gulf war, the "ownership" of news was in the hands of the military, not the media. The military dispensed and withheld whatever information it wished. Now that the war is over, the media industry is rapidly marketing this managed information through the sale of videotapes to the public. In the interest of economic gain, it seems, the media industry is willing to acquiesce to a process of information control and management lodged within the U.S. military.

Concerns about the ownership and marketing of knowledge are not limited to media institutions, however. The university has for some time been the instrument for creating and disseminating much of the knowledge which our society accepts as legitimate for addressing the significant issues of the day. The idea of the university as "the ivory tower" has often carried the negative connotation of privileged scholars tucked away from "real" life to contemplate issues with little or no relevance to public life at large. But it also conveys the possibility of an institution that can't be permeated by the globalizing forces that are deeply affecting other social institutions. It may therefore be a comforting idea for those who are alarmed about the implications of knowledge as property that the university remains a preserve of critical thinking, of free inquiry, a bastion of truth to counterbalance the potential effects of restricted, commodified, marketed bits of managed information.

Unfortunately, this comfort may be short-lived. The university as a repository of social knowledge that is preserved and developed in the public interest may be rapidly disappearing. In its place a new institutional form is emerging, distinguished by its ability to define its markets, cultivate entrepreneurial professors, attract corporate clients and secure intellectual property rights. The university is caught up in the same social, political and economic dynamic that has transformed the media and other social institutions.

In Canada, the term that has been developed by the Science Council of Canada to promote the objectives of this new institutional form is "the service university," though many features of the service university — and much of the public policy that aids its emergence — can be found in the United States, Great Britain, the countries of Western Europe and others whose economies are dependent on high-tech development. We can hardly criticize the idea that the *raison d'etre* of publicly funded institutions like the university should be "to serve," but the idea of "service" emerging in the universities of the 1990s represents a harnessing of the university's highly valued resources to very narrow and specialized objectives that benefit particular interests rather than society as a whole. "Service" in this case is simply another word for responding to the demands of the business sector. The term is not based on a holistic conception of the broad range of human needs — emotional, social, spiritual, political, intellectual, as well as economic — but rather the view that human progress is measured by economic growth and technological innovation.

The sites on which this "service university" is constructed have been primarily and initially the areas of technology transfer and scientific research. In exchange for financial support from corporate clients, universities and university scientists have become engaged in a wide range of corporate-university linking arrangements through which scientific research is more directly and deliberately concentrated on discoveries that will result in marketable products or technological breakthroughs that will enhance a corporation's competitive edge in the global market.

This linking of the university to a corporate impetus in order to fully exploit the benefits of the knowledge quest may appear on the surface to be a progressive development. But instead of making knowledge more widely available for socially useful purposes, the effect of this partnership is to control and limit knowledge dissemination. Knowledge that was free is now proprietary, and the production and marketing demands of corporations are the guiding force of scientific inquiry. Moreover, even though scientific and technological research have been the primary sites of these developments, the language and practices of the market and the primacy of "corporate relevance" have pervaded many if not most other academic disciplines, as well as the decision-making processes of the university itself.

For example, university "managers" increasingly see the communities that their institutions "serve" merely as markets to which they can target enrollment policies and curricular developments. They treat students as atomized "consumers" with specifiable needs, faculty and staff members as human resources whose specialized expertise and skills are distributable to a variety of necessary tasks. University buildings are physical plants whose profitability is to be enhanced at all costs, even if this results in crowded classrooms and no room at all for spontaneous interaction or unofficial (read "unapproved") university business. Moreover the buying and selling of the university's research resources to corporate bidders, and the marketing of intellectual property rights through patents, etc., have been accompanied by several unhappy results. These include an increase in secrecy among academic colleagues around their research activities, limiting the publication of research findings at least until patents have been secured, and skewing research objectives toward discoveries that conform to sponsor demands — what some have called a subversion of the scientific research process itself. The reader unfamiliar with these developments need only review some of the most recent headlines in American newspapers and newsmagazines concerning higher education and scientific research.

These results stand in stark and dramatic contrast to what has been of central importance to the university — the production of social knowledge — as well as to the image of the kind of place a university should (at least) aspire to be. Both in its public image and its internal practices, universities draw closer and closer to being corporate boardroom look-alikes rather than the free-thinking, open-to-spontaneity, diverse, exper-imental, risk-taking intellectual communities that some of us still imagine and believe in. The imposition of the "corporate model" on the university, as though it is the only organizational model available to us for achieving socially valuable purposes, creates bizarre distortions. The consequent perversion of the intellectual enterprise generates a profound cynicism not only in the faculty, many of whom have all too readily adopted an entrepreneurial approach to their work, but also in students who witness the deterioration of the quality of their education even while they are required to pay higher and higher tuition fees. At the heart of this perversion is the transformation of knowledge from being a social good to a marketable commodity.

The foundations of "the service university" can be traced back at least to the end of the Second World War. In the United States, the GI Bill sent thousands of young (mostly) men to college who would otherwise not have gone, and by the late 1950s and early 1960s most Western societies had begun to invest heavily in higher education. Universities expanded their facilities and boosted student enrollments. By the late 1960s, however, expansion had begun to give way to contraction as the political priority assigned to funding for education and other social programs was increasingly undermined by other economic demands. In Canada in the early 1980s, following a decade of fiscal retrenchment by the provincial governments (which have jurisdiction over education), both the provin-cial *and* federal governments, along with various research-funding and science-promoting organizations, began to articulate a "new direction" for universities.

This direction was first outlined in a report of the Corporate-Higher Education Forum, an organization founded in 1983 and consisting at the time of 25 university presidents and 25 top executives of major Canadian private corporations. (A similar organization was founded in the United States only a few years earlier.) The Forum's report, *Partnership for Growth*, contained a bold new proposal for solving the fiscal plight of Canadian universities: Heralding a new era of cooperation between corporations and universities, it argued that universities could solve the problems of underfunding by tuning their curricula and research pro-grams more directly to the needs of industry. Canada's corporations needed to be on the cutting edge of scientific breakthrough in order to compete in the new global economy, it argued, and by making available its knowledge-generating capacity to corporate clients who would be willing to pay for research, the university would acquire the funds needed to repair and update its facilities, to replenish its libraries, and to improve the quality of its educational programs.

Most important, perhaps, this proposal was intended as more than a marriage of convenience to get the university through some difficult times. The authors of the report strongly recommended that the provincial governments *continue* their underfunding policy — thus creating greater incentive in the university community to seek out corporate partners. Canadian universities were ripe for this suggestion, since throughout the 1970s and early 1980s they had become increasingly preoccupied with their ever shrinking share of public resources.

But ironically the drive for "efficiency" as a response to scarcity stimulated (and was used to justify) the growth of a more centralized managerial structure whose position in the university community gained in stature even as the budgetary situation worsened. Meanwhile the staff of the university — faculty and otherwise — responded to the effects of fiscal contraction by gaining collective bargaining rights, either through unionization or some form of special-plan bargaining. Though providing the means for protecting the staffs' previously acquired economic gains and involvement in decision-making, these developments also legiti-mized a space in the institution for "management" as a separate and distinct enterprise with the legal authority to make decisions. The com-bination of a centralized and more initiating management, along with a unionized and more marginalized academic staff, created within the university a greater receptivity — or vulnerability — to the idea of collaboration with corporate clients as a means of relieving financial stress.

This collaboration has taken a number of institutional forms: the creation of private companies that are owned and/or staffed by university professors and housed in university research labs and buildings; the development of "discovery parks" on university grounds to facilitate easy interchange between industrial and academic researchers; univer-sity offices of technology transfer; complex patent arrangements be-tween university researchers and corporate clients; and, in Canada, the establishment of "Centres of Excellence" that create a critical mass of scientific experts, both academic and industrial, in order to concentrate their research inquiries in areas that will lead to the development of marketable products. Those who support these developments say that money flows into the university either from corporate sponsors or from special government sources, usually in the form of "matched grants" that thereby further encourage universities to partner up with corporate clients. As well, universities may purchase shares in the private companies or claim royalties from patent applications.

Alongside these new institutional arrangements we also have a new form of intellectual worker, the "entrepreneurial professor," for whom the "ability to generate research funds" is the distinctive mark of honor. The typical entrepreneurial professor is an academic researcher who develops a marketable product — a genetic-engineering procedure, for example, or an instructional computer program — and secures venture capital from a corporate client in order to establish a private company to market the product. Often, both the university and the academic researcher will own shares in the company. Some prominent business leaders have argued that the granting of tenure should be based on an academic's income-generating record, and one university president recently proclaimed on public television his hope that all of his professors will engage in these profitable collaborations and become millionaires!

These developments are well along the way to changing the appearance of the Western university. But what also do they foster beneath the surface? For one thing, they have spawned a significant transformation in the organizational character of the university. Paradoxically, in spite of fiscal constraint, the size and scope of university administration has expanded exponentially in the last 20 years. From a president with a small support staff and several deans, university "administration" has become a high-powered team of managers — the president (often called the CEO), vice presidents, associate and assistant vice presidents, deans and associate deans. Each is supported by an expanded civil service of middle-level, professional-managerial personnel and clerical staff.

The centrality of management reflects the centrality of the budget in shaping the university's agenda, in which financial/management prerogatives supersede academic/professional concerns. "Efficiency," "productivity," "accountability" and "profitability" have taken the place of academic and educational criteria in setting priorities, allocating resources and developing institutional practices of all kinds. Moreover the institutional forms of corporate-university collaboration have sprung up outside of the academic collegial structure. In these endeavors, management works directly with collaborating researchers often around the edges of academic units like departments and faculty, and usually without being subject to the advice or direction of academic senates.

Taken together, financial constraint combined with corporate-university linkages are helping to transform a collegially directed academic organization into a managerially centralized administrative structure that delivers "services" to targeted markets and paying sponsors.

This institutional transformation has been premised on the expectation that the new income generated from more efficiently targeting resources to needs would assist the university in dealing with its deteriorating quality and inability to respond to demands. Ironically, however, the opposite appears to have happened. As Leonard Minsky and David Noble have argued concerning the situation in the United States, so it is our experience in Canada that this transformation has only exacerbated problems of quality and a deteriorating academic climate.

The fact is that the fiscal resources of the business community, not to mention its philanthropic sentiments, are nowhere near equal to the funding needs of the system of higher education. Furthermore, the kind of research that feeds the needs of new high-tech growth industries is extremely costly and creates a further financial drain on university resources. One way universities accommodate this drain is by allowing the teaching time of certain faculty to be bought out by research funds and assigning their teaching duties to part-time course directors at a much cheaper cost. Many undergraduates now complain that they have rarely if ever been taught by a full-time, continuing member of the university faculty during their years of study, and that the courses they had hoped to take have changed staff from year to year and therefore either lack stability or have been canceled altogether. In spite of the fact that universities have become themselves a market for the latest high-tech gimmickry and inventions, students neither feel that their own needs have any priority nor that the slick corporate appearance of many university offices represents any tangible improvement in their service delivery. Expensive, technological methods of administering various aspects of the university teaching enterprise — such as touch-tone telephone registration matched up with decrepit and virtually useless academic advising systems — leave students disgruntled and feeling neglected.

Libraries are still underbudgeted, and university buildings continue to deteriorate. Yet students are now being asked to pay ever increasing levels of tuition for a declining quality of educational service.

It is becoming clear that the economy of these business-university collaborations is not benefiting the university in the way that their promoters had promised. In the same way that Anthony Smith points to a "new economic system" becoming embedded in the media industry, so too the new economic order of the university has profound effects on the creation and dissemination of social knowledge. Academic researchers who look, or are driven, to private sector sponsors to fund their research must orient their interests toward marketable products, and more often than not the private sector sponsor then holds proprietary rights to the research findings. One study, for example, indicates that in the United States as much as one fourth of biotechnology research in higher education institutions is supported by industrial firms — meaning that the findings of this research are the property of the sponsors and cannot be published without their consent. Graduate students training with academic researchers may also be employees in the researcher's private company, and may be required to maintain secrecy, even to delay publication of their own theses, until the ownership of the knowledge they have helped to produce has been secured.

As well, a growing number of universities have proprietary interests in the scientific findings of faculty members. The potential for conflict of interest is obvious when it comes time for decisions about resource allocations to various departments, research units or individual academics. And in its efforts to maximize its profit margins and protect its financial interests, the university may be the very means of *closing off* rather than facilitating alternative or competing areas of inquiry, even though these areas may better serve the "public good."

It would be historically inaccurate to argue that the university's involvement in economic and technological development is only recent, brought on by the financial squeeze of the last 25 years. But it would also be a mistake to conclude that there is nothing new or especially startling about the turn of events we have outlined here. In a relatively short time universities have been virtually transformed from somewhat anarchically organized social institutions into fast-paced, strategically oriented businesses, a transformation that negates the earlier commitment to practices of free and open inquiry and collegial autonomy evident in many studies of universities carried out in the late 1960s and early '70s. The delivery of educational products and marketable information, preferably to the highest bidders, has been substituted for education and critical inquiry accessible to all who are able to benefit.

Some have blamed the recent decline of universities on a stagnating professoriate, protected from evaluation by tenure; a student body corrupted by vague and undisciplined themes such as women's studies, black studies and the like; and policies of accessibility and affirmative action that have led to the admission of too many inferior students. These critics have helped to sell the public on the idea that all of these problems can be resolved by a renewed commitment to "the pursuit of excellence."

But "excellence" is part of the problem. On the one hand, pursuing it by narrowing the pool of students who can gain entry will only reinstate an elitist university that restricts access to knowledge, even as it draws attention away from the very policies and practices that are narrowing and limiting the university's broad educational purposes. Moreover excellence itself has become a marketing strategy. Being able to successfully *create the image* of excellence is a major managerial undertaking, since universities must compete with each other for the limited financial resources of private donors. At our university, for example, even as the quality of education in the classroom deteriorates and campus services from the library to food are the subject of constant complaint, awards in "excellence" have been established in every area of campus activity imaginable. These awards become the basis for claiming that complaints about quality have been addressed even though the underlying causes of the problems, and the problems themselves, remain. Perhaps most ironic of all in this regard is the national award for excellence in business-education partnerships! Thus has excellence become a means of restricting, not expanding, the benefits of the university's quest for knowledge.

Over the years, universities have drawn fire from a number of quarters for legitimate reasons. They have often fostered disinterestedness in, and self-indulgent seclusion from, society's critical problems. They have often provided the means for disciplinarians to exercise an unaccountable monopoly over knowledge. They have contributed to the social inequalities that still pervade societies that claim to be the most progressive and democratic. It is easy enough for average citizens to let the university wallow in its own mud and not to be overly concerned about the possible demise of an all too privileged institution that has too long been unaccountable to its paying public.

But such a response is shortsighted. Universities are the public's resource in a world that increasingly relies on knowledge to inform, guide and direct its path. We don't argue for reinstating lost privileges, and we don't mourn for the return of a "golden era" when these hallowed institutions were free of corruption. We are not arguing that an outside contaminant has invaded the rarefied atmosphere of free inquiry and critical reflection. The erosion of the university's public purpose of creating and disseminating social knowledge is being aided and abetted from within as much as it is also being prompted from without. It is past time that a closer look be given to who is managing and controlling the university, and in whose interest.

Howard Buchbinder is an associate professor of social science, and Janice Newson an associate professor of sociology, both at York University in Toronto.

3

Acquiring an Alma Mater
or Achieving an Education

Thomas W. Bergmann

> . . . .*if we wish to become exact and fully fur-*
> *nished in any branch of knowledge which is*
> *diversified and complicated, we must consult*
> *the living man and listen to his living voice.*
> —Cardinal John Henry Newman in
> "What Is a University?"

It's painful to see angst on the face of a 17-year-old. Such a crippling emotion should not be allowed to conquer someone who has most of his life ahead of him, a future abundant with promise. Unfortunately, it was his awareness of what *is* ahead that led him to my door in the fall of 1990, bringing his angst and a copy of *U.S. News & World Report.*

When he showed me the magazine's cover, though, I understood why he felt as he did. The cover declared, "America's Best Colleges . . . Exclusive rankings of 450 universities and colleges." In the upper-left-hand corner, a seal-like design (as in "seal of approval") announced the companion "College Guide": a misnomer because the magazine contains no guide to the 450 institutions ranked, but rather several supplementary articles about recent trends in higher education. Inside the "seal" is an image of a diploma, and a second, much larger diploma dominates the center of the cover. The diplomas apparently symbolize, for *U.S. News,* the goal of attending a school highly ranked in its survey: to obtain a document certifying that the holder has graduated from a prestigious institution and is thus much more marketable than if he had not. Those images of the diploma give us our first clue about how *U.S. News* views higher education, and a close study of the survey confirms our suspicion.

The magazine even acknowledges, briefly, that part of its survey "is designed not to measure academic quality as such, but the academic reputations that have become so vital in opening doors after graduation — both to graduate school and to employment."

Hoping he would be enrolled in one of those "best" colleges next year, my visitor was beginning to make "the most important decision of my life" in the midst of his anxiety about how his decision will determine his future, and also in the midst of his parents' argument about the usefulness of the survey in his hand.

The young man — his name is Andy — had come to me because his parents are good friends of mine and he knew that I teach in a university's writing program (he has for some time been thinking about becoming a writer). He said he wanted me to help him decide where to go to college and, in so doing, resolve his parents' dispute over the *U.S. News* survey. At that point I began to feel a little angst of my own, because he was asking of me more than I could, or would, give him. His request reminded me of the confusion and cowardice that had short-circuited the intelligence and imagination I needed to enlighten my choosing of a university, back when my own future was more capacious than it is now. I told Andy that, although the decision must be his and I wouldn't intrude on his parents' advisory role, I would study the survey and report back to him.

My prior acquaintance with the *U.S. News* annual ranking was limited, the result of newspaper accounts of college presidents who either discounted its significance or dismissed it completely. On the surface the survey appears to be soundly conceived. *U.S. News* has selected five institutional attributes that it believes, when taken together, provide the most accurate measurement of the quality of American colleges and universities: academic reputation, student selectivity, faculty resources, financial resources and student satisfaction — all seemingly reasonable criteria for measurement. But what do they really measure, and how are the various measurements combined to rank the schools?

Each of these attributes is not only "scored" but also weighted in determining a school's ranking. *U.S. News* weights them as follows: academic reputation, student selectivity and faculty resources, 25 percent each; financial resources, 20 percent; and student satisfaction, 5 percent.

U.S. News arrives at the "academic reputation" score by means of a questionnaire sent to 4,151 college presidents, deans and admissions officers. The "financial resources" score is determined by "the 1989 dollar total of [the school's] educational and general expenditures, divided by its total enrollment." "Student satisfaction" is measured by "the average percentage of the 1982 to 1984 freshman classes who graduated within five years of the date they enrolled." The scores for the other two attributes — "student selectivity" and "faculty resources" — are derived by totalling additional scores of subcomponent attributes.

In regard to "student selectivity" (this means the school's selectivity in choosing its students, not vice versa), the subcomponents are "the acceptance rate (the percentage of applicants who were accepted); the 'yield' (the percent of those accepted who actually enrolled); high school class standings; and either the average combined scores on the Scholastic Aptitude Test or the composite American College Testing Assessment." Finally, in regard to "faculty resources," the subcomponents are "[the] ratio of full-time students to full-time faculty; the percentage of full-time faculty with doctorates; the percentage of faculty with part-time status; and the average salary, including fringe benefits, for tenured full professors."

In other words, scores from 11 categories ultimately determine the school's rank, which raises a question about whether such statistical complexity might obfuscate rather than elucidate. But *U.S. News* provides an exhaustive explanation of its methodology in order to impress the reader with its painstaking attempts to ensure accuracy. The magazine even goes so far as to presume an endorsement from the nation's "best" university. The introduction states that, in a speech made by Derek Bok, former president of Harvard (ranked number one in 1990's survey), he acknowledged "the difficulty of measuring educational quality"; then it quotes him as saying, " . . .many students do not care enough to ferret out the scraps of information that *are* available . . . [nor do they] exert an informed pressure that forces universities to make determined, comprehensive efforts to improve their educational programs." To which the magazine responds, "*U.S. News* believes that this sixth survey of *America's Best Colleges* provides much of the information Bok feels students should have."

I doubt it. *U.S. News'* information simply does not accomplish what the magazine implies it does. In fact, the magazine's subtle manipulation of Bok's remarks tells us far more about this survey than its self-satisfied disquisition on methodology. The survey's five key attributes (and eight subcomponents) may tell us some facts about the institutions, but in regard to helping a prospective undergraduate determine the quality of education he or she could achieve there, they have either dubious value or none at all.

For example, *U.S. News* measures "student satisfaction" solely on the basis of the graduation rate, an absurd simplification of the myriad reasons why students do or do not remain in the schools they enrolled in. One can see, however, why the magazine needed to concoct such a statistic, albeit clumsily: the parents of prospective students are the primary marketing target of this survey. Yet *U.S. News* insults the eventual consumers of the product by weighting this attribute the lowest: 5 percent. If students are so important, why is their satisfaction so unimportant? The reason for this paradox, one supposes, is that the magazine, while insisting that this attribute be included, knows it to be worthless as defined and thus gives it such a low weight to prevent it from doing more serious damage to the rest of the statistical machinery. The method of weighting is itself questionable; the assignment of percentages to the various attributes is totally arbitrary, but surely affects the final result. The ludicrousness of this attribute is plainly evident in the ranking. The survey's top five universities are Harvard, Stanford, Yale, Princeton and the California Institute of Technology. Their student satisfaction scores are, respectively, 6, 11, 2, 2, and 31. What is one to make of that? If Harvard is the best university, why don't its students know that? And do students who enroll at Yale just happen to be a lot easier to please than their counterparts at Cal Tech?

The "financial resources" attribute is equally meaningless and, as with "student satisfaction," its inclusion in the ranking is plainly consumer-oriented: "Look, Dad, Harvard's spending $46,918 on me this year. It's like we're making a profit on the tuition we have to pay." The significant issue is not how much money is spent per student, but how the money is spent. How much goes to scholarships? Which educational programs are properly funded and which shortchanged? How much goes to faculty salaries, and in which disciplines, and at which ranks? One subcomponent scores the average salary for tenured full professors. A more revealing statistic would be the percentage of the faculty salary budget allocated to the junior ranks, to which the recruitment of promising younger professors involves the fiercest competition in the academic marketplace.

The "faculty resources" attribute, although based on some useful criteria (faculty/student ratio, percentage of faculty with Ph.D.s), fails to answer an important question: Does the institution's senior faculty teach freshmen and sophomores? And the survey is incapable of answering an even more important question: What is the quality of teaching at the institution, in each department, in each classroom?

Although the *U.S. News* ranking does not pay any attention to the single most critical factor determining the quality of a student's education, college presidents are beginning to pay a good deal more attention to it. In one of the supplemental articles, Hunter Rawlings, president of the University of Iowa and a member of a panel investigating the quality of teaching at the undergraduate level at 58 major research institutions, is quoted as saying, "It comes down to parents in Iowa asking whether they should be paying, say, another 5 percent if their children are not going to be taught by full-time faculty members in their first two years." Another encouraging indication of this growing awareness of the primacy of teaching is a Syracuse University program intended to give more weight to teaching when deciding matters of salary increases and tenure.

Of the ranking's five key attributes, the most disturbing one is the "exclusive *U.S. News* reputational survey." The magazine admits that this attribute "is not designed to measure academic quality" (as though the others are), and only 60 percent of the presidents, deans and directors of admissions responded: a "record" (which raises even greater doubt about the significance of the five previous surveys). That response also suggests how university officials value the survey. Furthermore, one wonders whether the respondents represented primarily highly or lowly ranked institutions, or institutions not ranked at all. It also seems probable that, whatever they thought of when they did respond, it was more likely senior faculty scholarship and research than undergraduate teaching — yet the survey is intended to benefit prospective undergraduates.

This highly subjective survey provides one of the three attributes to which *U.S. News* assigns the most weight (25 percent), and we infer that this survey is the only justification for that eye-catching "Exclusive" on the magazine's cover; all the other information is supplied by the schools. In other words, the attribute given the most weight and the greatest fanfare is the one almost half of the educators polled didn't consider worth responding to. Exclusive, indeed.

But that word, so prominently placed on the cover, is as revealing as it is misleading. It misleads because the annual ranking is not "exclusive" in the sense of a scoop: most of the information is available at the institutions, and there are other similar surveys. Even the reputational survey is "exclusive" only in the pejorative sense. Yet *U.S. News'* choice of that word is also revealing. It was probably chosen because it speaks so persuasively to the obviously large audience identified by the magazine as wanting exactly this kind of ranking.

If I were a prospective undergraduate, I would include Harvard among the schools to which I applied, because were I accepted I would have the advantage of sitting in a classroom and listening to whatever teachers such as Robert Coles or Stephen Jay Gould or Seamus Heaney or Helen Vendler had to say to me. On the other hand, many prospective undergraduates (or maybe their parents) would choose Harvard because they think being an alumnus of Harvard (if only with a baccalaureate degree) would give them certain "advantages," perhaps in obtaining a "better" job in the "best" firm, and obtaining entree in "certain" social circles (if the place in which they found themselves were consequential enough to have them). I happen to think that such prospects are more mythological than realistic, especially for the holder of a B.A., but I also happen to think that those who believe the myth are legion.

If I were to measure the quality of Robert Coles' teaching, or that of all of his peers at the 449 other institutions, I could not do it with *U.S. News'* method. I would need words, lots of words, far more words than anyone would take the time to read. There are, of course, other ways in which prospective students and their parents can discern the quality of education — the quality of teaching — at the schools they're interested in. But those other ways involve doing research of one kind or another, and that takes time, too. *U.S. News* knows that the readers who depend on its survey — who buy its survey — don't have the time to read too many words or do research on their own. So *U.S. News* does it with numbers. They can be understood so much more quickly, so much more easily. There's no gray area with numbers. In a ranking, number one is better than number 450. Everyone knows that. And everyone knows that being as close to number one as you can possibly get is where you want to be, whether it's a college or a career position, a neighborhood or a country club. Everyone knows what a number means, even if they don't know why.

It is not surprising, then, that *U.S. News* knows that using numbers to tell people who number one is, and who is close to number one, will sell magazines. And so does its survey's corporate sponsor.

Somehow, this whole business reminds me of Annie Dillard's anecdote of the male butterfly: "A wonderful entomological experiment shows that a male butterfly will ignore a living female butterfly of his own species in favor of a painted cardboard one, if the cardboard one is big. If the cardboard one is bigger than he is, bigger than any female butterfly ever could be, bigger than four female butterflies, he jumps the piece of cardboard. Over and over again, he jumps the piece of cardboard. Nearby, the real, living female butterfly opens and closes her wings in vain."

When Herb and Lucy heard that their son had paid me a visit, they invited me over to their home so that we might relax over dinner and chat a bit about Andy's dilemma. It wasn't a particularly relaxing evening, and Herb and Lucy did most of the chatting, very little of which I have the energy to recall. Andy started out the discussion by saying that he didn't really know where he wanted to go or what he wanted to major in. "I think I just want what I guess would be called a liberal education." I told him that sounded good to me, although I sometimes call it a liberating education. "Liberating from what?" Herb asked, a little testily. I said, "From thinking what other people think, for one thing."

For some reason, that set them off. Lucy launched her attack on the *U.S. News* survey, and Herb did his best to defend it. Finally, she aimed her main complaint at her husband and fired: "You talk as though education is a product. That's what annoys me most about this survey. *U.S. News* seems to think a college — or more to the point, an education — is something you can buy and bring home, like a VCR that got a top rating in *Consumer Reports*. In fact, now that I think of it, that's exactly what this survey reminds me of, with all those columns and numbers and statistics and painstaking explanations of the 'scientific' methods of measurement they used, all to convince you of its unimpeachable authority."

She turned to me and asked if I agreed. I tried to say that I did, in a way that wouldn't offend Herb, who sincerely wants what is best for his son. But after listening to their argument in the mute and forlorn company of Andy, I abandoned my initial reluctance to get involved in the debate. I told him as I left that the next day I would give him some expert counsel about what to consider when choosing a college, and when attending one, too.

The expert counsel I had in mind is contained in an essay to which the matter of the *U.S. News* survey had sent me back, as though to the healing waters. Cardinal John Henry Newman wrote "What Is a University?" in 1851, after being appointed rector of the new Catholic University proposed for Dublin. Cardinal Newman's definition of a university contrasts vividly with the definition implicit in the *U.S. News* survey. Not surprisingly, so does his method. *U.S. News* teases us with its manipulation of misleading statistics; Cardinal Newman teaches us with his mastery of the high style in English prose. And one of his metaphors ought to attract advocates of *U.S. News'* approach to his:

> [Whenever people are] serious about getting what, in the language of trade, is called 'a good article,' when they aim at something precise, something refined, something really luminous, something really large, something choice, they go to another market [than books]; they avail themselves [of] the ancient method, of oral instruction, of present communication between man and man, . . . of the personal influence of a master, and the humble initiation of a disciple.

For Newman, the quality of a student's education derives not from the institution but from the individual interactions of its faculty with its students. A corollary truth, ignored by *U.S. News*, is perhaps even more important: The quality of a student's education has as much to do with the student as with his teachers. The *Consumer Reports* approach that *U.S. News* uses to rank institutions is incapable of ranking the quality of education, because an institution (however you choose to evaluate it) is not the education you *might* be able to achieve there. You can't consume an education, but you might consummate one.

And consummating an education requires both "the personal influence of a master" and "the humble initiation of a disciple." The best education can occur either frequently or rarely in a given institution. But it *only* occurs when a productive collaboration takes place between a particular student and a particular teacher, a teacher who may not be one of the school's most distinguished scholars or most heavily funded researchers (although they are the ones who have much to do with an institution's reputation).

In short, true education occurs when there is, as between Newman's master and disciple, "a sympathy of mind with mind":

> [No] book can convey the special spirit and delicate peculiarities of its subject with that rapidity and certainty which attend on the sympathy of mind with mind, through the eyes, the look, the accent, and the manner, in casual expression thrown off at the moment, and the unstudied turns of familiar conversation.

A major implication of what Newman is saying would doubtless seem subversive to advocates of the *U.S. News* approach, but it is inescapable: The best education is, to a great extent, fortuitous. No high school senior can predict which "living voice" will rouse him from the drowsy self-preoccupation of adolescence; awaken him to an appreciative understanding of himself and of the world around him; encourage him to wean himself from the security of inherited or borrowed ideas and attitudes; demonstrate for him that thinking, in Robert Frost's words, "is just putting this and that together"; and exhort him as he educates himself into a fruitful engagement with the world. No high school senior can predict who will be the ones to do that *for him*. He ought to be reassured, however, that at least a few of them can be found at almost any one of the 450 institutions in the *U.S. News* survey.

But is only a few too few? Ask a graduate of any college or university to recall those teachers who enabled him to be *in* the world — confronting the mysteries of which he is a part — in ways that invigorated and transformed him. No list of such teachers, I wager, would contain more than a few names. I also wager that the feelings evoked by the alma mater, whatever it is, would be far more ambivalent than the feelings evoked by those few names.

James Dickey once said, "The main thing that a teacher can do for a student is . . . confirm the student in his desire to take [the field of study] seriously." When I decided to do advanced work in English, I returned to my alma mater so that I could work with the professor who, in my undergraduate days, had confirmed me in my desire to take literature seriously. But when I told him what area I wanted to specialize in (it was one of his areas), he said "Oh well, then you'll want to work with Professor _____." He was referring to an internationally known scholar who eventually moved from that institution (which is ranked in the top 25 by *U.S. News*) to another (ranked in the top five), and finally to one of England's great universities, where he held an endowed chair. The professor to whom I was speaking recommended his senior, more famous colleague with what he thought to be my best interest in mind. I told him that I was well aware of the other's reputation but that I had come back so that we could work together, and thus we did. I was moved by my professor's humility, which strengthened my conviction that I had made the right choice. Surely Cardinal Newman would agree that such humility distinguishes the true master, just as it governs the true disciple.

I told this story to Andy, noting that it supported my view that the best education is largely fortuitous; I had invested virtually no time or effort in the selection of my undergraduate institution. But I quickly added that, if he wanted to maximize his chance of gaining an education that would be of the most value to him, he would have to do some extensive research. He should try to find schools that have faculty strength in the areas of study that would best prepare him for the two or three futures that at the moment seemed most likely to him. I also suggested that he visit as many of those schools as he could, to determine whether he would feel comfortable there. Finally, of course, he had Cardinal Newman's essay.

After reading the essay, Andy reported back to me to tell me what he thought. He said he was impressed, and he pointed out several passages that he especially liked. This was his favorite:

> [A university] is the place to which a thousand schools make contributions; in which the intellect may safely range and speculate, sure to find its equal in some antagonist activity, and its judge in the tribunal of truth. It is a place where inquiry is pushed forward and discoveries verified and perfected, and rashness rendered innocuous, and error exposed, by the collision of mind with mind, and knowledge with knowledge. It is the place where the professor becomes eloquent, and is a missionary and a preacher, displaying his science in its most complete and its most winning form, pouring it forth with the zeal of enthusiasm, and lighting up his own love of it in the breasts of his hearers.

"But it does sound kind of idealistic," he added. I said I thought it probably seemed idealistic because in this country we are accustomed to thinking of a college education as being what we need to get a good job. In Newman's view, education has quite a different purpose, which is elegantly made evident in that passage. Another reason it seems idealistic is that the kind of teacher Newman describes in his last sentence is encountered too infrequently by students in today's colleges and universities. But that kind of teacher does exist. Because of Andy's interest in writing, I gave him some examples of how the personal influence of a master provided crucial guidance to several important American writers as they were beginning to develop their craft and art.

Andy has kept me posted on his deliberations; he seems to be on the right track. He is also fortunate to have concerned parents who articulate such clearly opposing views of higher education. When Andy finally comes through their "antagonist activity" to his decision, he will have taken a major step toward achieving the education he seeks. And if he continues to use life's antagonist activities to educate himself into his own right way of being in the world, he will qualify for membership in the most exclusive club there is. Its annual dues will require from him far more than the initial entrance fee and will be exacted from him in a far more precious currency: the diligence of mind and heart.

Thomas W. Bergmann is a free-lance writer and part-time lecturer in English in the division of continuing education at Northwestern University.

4

Gumshoes at the Gates

Richard M. Cyert

I learned about the university and the media early in my career as a university president. A reporter whom I knew engaged me in conversation, and, as is my wont, I spoke freely, frankly and unflatteringly about a wealthy member of the community who held rather extreme political positions. I thought it was a conversation between friends; he thought of it, as it turned out, as an interview: I read his story the next day with my quotes prominently displayed. Thus did I learn that one has to treat representatives of the media carefully.

The experience also made clear to me that the lifeblood of a university, particularly a private one, is favorable publicity. The university's ability to raise money and to attract students will depend to a great extent on its ability to become known in its market as an institution of significance in teaching, research or both. For the national research university, that market is a large geographical area.

Of course many elements determine a university's quality — administration, faculty, students, staff, physical plant, financial strength, admissions office, financial aid office, student affairs office, development and public relations — and a university president who wants an effective organization cannot ignore any part of the system.

Ironically, the element that presidents frequently *do* ignore is perhaps the most important: media relations. Particularly if they have come through the academic ranks, many presidents mistakenly believe that the quality of their faculty is the sole determinant of the quality of their institutions. Unfortunately, the world is not that simple. A university may be the best in the world in terms of its education, research and faculty, but if no one hears about them other than by word of mouth, the university will suffer.

For years academic administrators have used the term "media" as though it implied a homogeneous mass, a use that is clearly inexact. For universities there are important national newspapers — primarily the *New York Times* and the *Wall Street Journal* — and local ones; as well as news services; weekly newsmagazines; special-interest publications such as *Scientific American*; plus radio and television, both local and national. Some of these media serve the same purpose as far as the university is concerned, but for the most part they contribute differently to its needs. For the research university, the national publications are the most useful in recruiting a geographically diverse student body and in enabling the university to extend its fund raising to people and corporations over a broad area. National stories, whatever the medium, also help authenticate the school's claim to excellence among its students, faculty and alumni.

The local media, by contrast, help strengthen ties at home. Every national university draws at least a quarter of its students from its home state, and similarly at least 15 to 25 percent of its funds. Local stories that reach large concentrations of alumni help keep them friendly and contributing, and they also help sustain the morale of the faculty. (Despite a faculty's general apprehension about publicity, and sometimes outright hostility to it, they are nonetheless impressed with public attention.)

To attract students, a university may merely need its name in the paper frequently. There are instances, for example, where colleges that have reaped publicity from success in a high-profile sport such as football or basketball have had a significant spurt in their applications for admission (though it is not clear how many qualified applicants were involved or what the final impact of those spurts was on enrollment). It is not as clear that such publicity will help a school in its fund raising, and in any case the nation's major research universities are not, for the most part, athletic powers, and so they strive instead for national and international media attention that reflects the quality of their science and scholarship. A university becomes known for doing good work in particular areas, and this kind of attention allows a president or development officer to approach corporations or foundations with which the university has had little or no previous interaction.

The media, on the other hand, are extremely interested in news about the university. Particularly where universities are located in urban areas, the actions associated with them are always of great interest to the people who live there, and therefore the local media attempt to cover these activities in detail.

More importantly, however, the public's interest in higher education — if not its stake — has grown significantly in recent years as knowledge has become the primary ingredient for economic development, a trend that will only grow stronger. Even now America's universities are among the few national institutions with a positive balance of trade: Many more foreign students come to study here, particularly in our research universities, than do Americans study abroad. At the same time that a university is pleased to get media attention, the media clearly are getting news that is important to their readers and viewers.

In this respect the whole process plays into the hands of the university's public relations staff, and their efforts lead to greater public activity on the part of the president. University presidents make trips for interviews with reporters and editors of national publications in media centers such as New York, Washington, D.C., Chicago and Los Angeles. Additionally, presidents are often encouraged by their public relations staffs to write op-ed articles. A "think piece" in a national publication is a coup for the school.

At one level, then, the relationship between the university and the media is a mutually beneficial one. Both parties stand to benefit in the bargain.

At another level, however, the relationship is sour. Like many people, reporters have a preconceived notion of what they are going to see in universities and, as a result, see what they wish to. There was a time not too long ago, for example, when many reporters were convinced that a research relationship between universities and corporations was essentially destructive to the university; research done with corporate money might be kept as proprietary, researchers might not be permitted to publish their findings nor the public to benefit from them. When a reporter came to Carnegie Mellon and found he had to get special permission to enter a particular area, he immediately deduced that there was an unhealthy secret involved, and, without further investigation, concluded that he had stumbled onto a "sensational" story. In fact, the entrance requirements were there because a corporation had let the university use advanced equipment that had not yet been put on the market and did not want its competitors to see it. Eventually the research was made public and became the basis for some significant advances in computer usage.

Many other university presidents, I'm sure, have had similar experiences. My own conclusion is that if these experiences have created an adversarial relationship between the university and the media, the fault lies largely on the media's side of the ledger: The problem is poor reporting. The reporter simply does not perform the investigative process adequately, an occurrence that seems to happen more frequently with universities than with other institutions. Why? One possibility, borne out by research, may be that inexperienced reporters are broken in on the educational beat. This practice is one that begs examination, as it greatly hinders public understanding of the role of the university.

Faculty members, for example, are not always eager or even willing to cooperate in the media-university relationship. There is a general feeling among them that mainstream publicity is not really appropriate to scholarship, even that it is somewhat demeaning. But a far more significant reason for faculty reluctance is their fear of being misquoted or having their research results distorted. Few newspapers have science reporters skilled enough to understand research in the natural, biomedical or social sciences, or engineering. Reporters are also frequently deficient in their ability to listen and record faithfully, and thus it often happens that research results are reported to be more definitive than they actually are, or made to appear as though they have more relevance for some social malady than in fact they do. Such distortions are harmful in several respects, not least in the sheer embarrassment of having one's research appear to claim implications that one's peers will realize are false. A related and more serious problem is that such stories may harm a researcher's chances of getting further funding from granting agencies, although most are sophisticated enough to ignore unrealistic claims that appear in newspapers.

Another area of difficulty between the university and the press is not unique to the enterprise of higher education, and that is secrecy. A university is particularly interested in maintaining secrecy, for example, when its trustees are searching for a new president or some other officer in the organization. There is always concern that a candidate who has a position elsewhere will be adversely affected if the candidacy becomes public knowledge, and a university that makes every effort to guard against that possibility will get the best pool of available candidates. But invariably there will be some reporters who think themselves aggressive, perceptive sleuths in the mold of Woodward and Bernstein, a development that only exacerbates pressure in an institutional setting where it is notoriously difficult to maintain secrecy in the first place.

Reporters' investigative aspirations have occasionally also resulted in destructive and time-consuming public controversies for universities, particularly public ones. Consider, for example, the recent great to-do made over presidential and professorial salaries. Because of the IRS requirements that nonprofits report the five highest-paid individuals on their payrolls, and because of the Freedom of Information Act, these data have become available to the press, and disclosure stories have appeared in virtually every newspaper in the country that has a university in town or close by and in many of the national publications covering education. Invariably the "hook" for these stories has been that the president is not always the highest-paid person in the university; rather a medical school professor or some professor of engineering or computer science is earning more. (It's worth pointing out here that some prominent journalists make considerably more than their editors or producers — and the difference is often more attributable to their stature as "celebrities" than their abilities as journalists.) These stories are invalidated by the fact that some presidents, including me, have deferred-income plans that are not open to everyone in the university, and so their salaries look lower in comparison to others' than they actually are. Reporters, however, delighted with their find, rarely bother to look beyond the surface figures. Worse, neither they nor their editors question the relevance of their story, if any, to the operation or purposes of the university. (On the other hand, my low salary evoked great sympathy from many faculty members, many of whom were further moved by the fact that I had not tried to escalate it.)

Another ready source of "news" seems to be student behavior, which with some frequency and predictability will be contrary to accepted norms. Their behavior may be political or social, serious, silly or abhorrent, but these activities, particularly when they have sexual or racial overtones, are immediately seized upon by the news media as fodder for the front page. These stories get attention completely out of proportion to their importance and become a source of embarrassment to the administration and damage to the reputation of the university. I suffered through a number of such incidents, but the condom party stands out in memory. As part of a sexual awareness week, the students held a party in which condoms were used in a wide variety of decorative ways, and of course the celebration was covered in detail by the local media and then beamed nationwide by a wire service. For weeks thereafter my mail box was filled with letters from distraught alumni. (Somehow the alumni who have given little or nothing to the university tend to be the ones who always threaten to stop giving.)

Naturally such stories create feelings of hostility between the university and the press. University officials reason that even though they have been cooperative on important stories and make faculty members available when the press needs an expert, when the news media have an opportunity to exploit a story with negative consequences for the university, they run with it.

Obviously it is easy to forget that the press has a responsibility to give what it considers news to the public, and certainly any news with an element of sensationalism in it is appealing to most readers. Thus from the standpoint of the press and other media managers, they are only doing their job. They also see this kind of reporting as distinct from the coverage that the university wants and may even seek. It is only after a president has experienced a few of these situations and realizes that the stories were not as damaging as they seemed — and that nothing is deader than yesterday's newspaper — that he or she can take such stories in stride.

People in universities, particularly presidents, tend to believe that universities should not be viewed like any other institution subject to investigative journalism. Faculty and administrators alike believe they are there because their motives are generally intellectual and nonmaterialistic, yet the typical investigative attitude assumes their motivation is no different from people at for-profit organizations. I understand that position; I sympathize with it and even held it while I was president. However, the fact is that in a democracy no institution can be sacrosanct. As we have seen only recently with stories about fraudulent data in scientific articles, peculiar charges in overhead calculations, and various college sports scandals, universities occasionally need to be held accountable by the media. But journalists who wish to turn an investigative eye on higher education need to be better trained than they presently are, and they need to make a significant commitment of time. One interview with a disgruntled employee cannot be the basis for an exposé. Education is a complex and difficult story to cover and cannot be left to novices. It should not be viewed as a place to break in new reporters who, once they've gained a little experience, can be transferred to the business desk.

The simplistic approach that so many media bring to their coverage of higher education is nowhere better exemplified than in the annual college rating game, an endeavor not unlike the business of rating football or basketball teams and about as questionable. Obviously a complex organization such as a university defies simple ranking by a single number, and there is no win-loss record to use in judging it. There can be large qualitative discrepancies between the university as a research organization and as a teaching one, and as well between its various departments and colleges. There can be large discrepancies in the way individual universities are financed, too; some have large endowments while others may receive large amounts in gifts.

This, however, does not hinder or obstruct the media from attempting the Herculean task of "rating" them, nor does the folly of the effort prevent prospective students and parents from taking such ratings seriously. Being included in the top 10 or top 30 can have a positive effect on admission applications, and not being included a negative one. Thus university administrators, despite their view of the foolishness of such ratings, are forced to pay attention to the criteria that guide them. Many try to improve the criteria, but others allow themselves to be influenced by them to the point of distraction, intent on improving their ranking.

The media, to be fair about it, are simply attempting to meet a need. Many families, particularly those with first-generation students going off to college, do not have reliable information with which to make a decision. Frequently, guidance counselors in the high schools are not adequately informed either, and so the media's ratings tend to carry, by default, an authority out of all proportion to their validity. At the same time it must be said that the college-rating business has been a lucrative sideline for those who engage in it; we are all familiar with the new-and-improved guides to colleges that pop up in bookstores each spring. This kind of "packaging" only reinforces my view that, for the most part, the media have a poor understanding of what higher education is about.

There is no question that a university must have good relations with the media. If anything, the university needs the media more than they need the university; press attention is vital for the health of any institution.

But the media *do* need the university, and their need will grow stronger as the public recognizes the role that universities play in promoting economic development. Higher education is a constant source of interesting stories, ranging from medical discoveries and robotic constructions for space exploration to cultural commentary and pronouncements on public policy. But the larger story of the university — its role in economic development and its contributions to the cultural life of the community — rarely if ever gets media attention, and here the university must take the initiative itself. It must encourage media respect by being as open as possible, and it must clearly — and often — articulate its role in enriching the life of the community and the nation.

Richard M. Cyert is president emeritus of Carnegie Mellon University.

5

The "Ivy Leaguers": News Shapers and the National Media

Lawrence C. Soley

Iraq invaded Kuwait too late for the Eastern edition of the August 1, 1990, network evening news. During the ABC newscast, anchor Peter Jennings did tell viewers that talks between Kuwait and Iraq to resolve their differences had broken down. Neither Dan Rather nor Tom Brokaw mentioned Iraq or Kuwait in their newscasts.

But the news did not come too late for "Nightline," which hurriedly rounded up what in the succeeding months became the "usual suspects": Columbia University professor Gary Sick, Georgetown University professor Anthony Cordesman, and the Brookings Institution's Judith Kipper. ABC News hired Cordesman and Kipper as consultants for their news programs, to provide backgrounders for reporters and appear on camera for newscasts. ABC also hired retired Admiral William Crowe (who in later Senate testimony would caution against going to war) and retired Lieutenant General Bernard Trainor as military consultants. Crowe was chairman of the Joint Chiefs of Staff and an adviser to Presidents Reagan and Bush before retiring from the military in 1989. Trainor worked as military correspondent for the *New York Times* after retiring from the U.S. Marines, and is currently director of the national security program at Harvard and a board member of the Institute for Foreign Policy Analysis, a Massachusetts-based think tank.

CBS signed up retired Generals George Crist and Michael Dugan as military consultants; NBC retained retired Lieutenant General William Odom. CBS also relied on its longtime Middle East consultant, Johns Hopkins University professor Fouad Ajami, for background and political analysis of events in the Middle East. Council on Foreign Relations Senior Fellow Richard Murphy, a former ambassador and assistant secretary of state for the Near East, provided similar analysis for NBC.

Cordesman, Trainor, Ajami, Murphy and Kipper were some of the more visible "news shapers" of the war — individuals who provide background and analysis about news events for the national broadcast networks but are not themselves news makers. These high-profile news shapers come primarily from think tanks, the elite media, or select, private universities in the East, and many are former government officials or advisers. Regardless of the issue, network reporters and Washington correspondents rely on news shapers affiliated with these institutions, the same ones that C. Wright Mills described as part of the self-conscious "power elite." "People are either accepted into this class or they are not," Mills wrote. "Members know one another, see one another socially and at business, and so, in making decisions, take one another into account."

During the U.S. invasion of Panama in December 1989, for example, retired Admiral Eugene Carroll of the Center for Defense Information, a Washington think tank, shaped news for ABC; and political analysis for the networks was provided by American University professor William LeoGrande and Columbia University professor Henry Graff. During previous coverage of events in Central America, network reporters turned to Columbia University professor Pamela Falk and Johns Hopkins University professor Riordan Roett for expert analysis. Conspicuously absent from network news programs were professors from public universities within the Trump shuttle corridor — which runs from Boston to Washington — and scholars from colleges located elsewhere in the country.

There are neither shortages of public universities within the Trump shuttle corridor — the University of Maryland, Rutgers, Temple and the City University of New York, to name a few — nor shortages of experts at universities outside it. But few are ever asked to shape the news, particularly news of international affairs.

Although national journalists may go to a broad range of institutions for backgrounders, they almost invariably turn to experts from a few select institutions to appear on camera or for colorful quotes. Those experts who appear constantly are on a "Golden Rolodex" — along with the names of think tank analysts, elite academics and ex-public officials. This reliance on elites once prompted New York Senator Daniel Patrick

Moynihan to characterize Washington reporters as "Ivy Leaguers." For them, he says, "journalism has become, if not an elite profession, a profession attracted to elites."

This situation isn't the result of a conspiracy, though at one level it has some obvious chummy aspects to it. The national media make extensive use of experts, whether as members of editorial boards or as sources or both — an organization like CNN, for example, lists some 700 academics as experts on a variety of subjects. Most never appear on camera, though they may be instrumental in shaping the news. But generally speaking the degree of their expertise isn't the media's concern, as the experts themselves are often acutely aware. The media are less concerned with the accuracy of their predictions or the subtlety of their analyses than they are with having the semblance of a debate. Indeed, the people most suited to life in the Golden Rolodex are those who, in the words of Hodding Carter III, can "echo conventional wisdom in well-tuned phrases that neither disturb nor illuminate. . . . To be considered unconventional, eccentric or 'extreme' is more to be feared in these circles than to be proved wrong." In such a system what the experts say and the strength of their analyses are far less important to the media than their institutional affiliations.

The national media's infatuation with academics from a few elite universities may stem in part from their eagerness to give an authoritative imprimatur to an issue. A commentator from Yale with a strongly "liberal" point of view, for example, poses less risk from a network's point of view than, say, a scholar with the same views from the University of Iowa. Yale, Harvard, Georgetown and a few others all have name recognition, the thinking goes, and so they give instant credibility to a story.

If the issue is law, for instance, the media will call Harvard University law professors Laurence Tribe and Alan Dershowitz, or Georgetown University professors Barry Carter and Paul Rothstein, or a handful of others. If a Supreme Court case originated in the Midwest or far West, reporters *might* call law professors from one of four other private universities: the University of Chicago, Northwestern, Stanford or the University of Southern California.

Importantly, "name recognition" isn't necessarily the media's creation. Increasingly universities or schools within them have been actively courting reporters, holding programs and making their people available for comment. Johns Hopkins has been conspicuously successful in this regard, for example, but other institutions have made significant publicity gains as well. Only a few universities, notably the well-known Ivies, have name recognition that rivals Kleenex — though they, too, pay great attention to public relations.

Anyone who watches the national media closely for a period of time senses intuitively that a disproportionate number of academic experts come from these few "elite" universities. Fairness and Accuracy in Reporting, the liberal media watchdog group, has attributed this skewed selection of sources to conservative political biases of corporate media. But if that is an issue (and I believe it is), it fails to account for, or even address, the extensive reliance of reporters in New York and Washington on experts from a few elite, private universities. If journalists preferred political conservatives to liberals, for example, they would have interviewed neoconservative scholar Irving Louis Horowitz about Latin America rather than liberal professor William LeoGrande; and Princeton University professor Stephen Cohen, who once penned articles for *The Nation*, would not have become the media presence that he is. The same can be said of Columbia's Edward Said, a frequent commentator on Middle East affairs whose strong views about Palestinian self-determination are often unsettling for liberals and conservatives both. Conservative critics who assert that the media are liberally biased likewise have a difficult time explaining the frequent appearances of ex-Republican officials and political conservatives like Anthony Cordesman, William Hyland, Dimitri Simes and Edward Luttwak.

The national media's reliance on experts from a few elite universities has deprived the public of the views of some of the United States' leading authorities in several fields. With respect to Latin America, for example, few are more knowledgeable than Horowitz, James Petras and Maurice Zeitlin. A comparison of citations in the *Social Science Citation Index*, a publication that tracks the references appearing in 1,500 scholarly journals, shows that Petras, who teaches at the State University of New York at Binghamton, is cited more frequently by other Latin America experts than any other scholar. He has also written or edited 15 books on South and Central America, more than any of the experts to whom Washington reporters go for their sound bites. Rutgers University professor and *Society* magazine editor Horowitz is one of America's leading political sociologists, and both he and UCLA professor Zeitlin have written extensively on Latin American politics and society. Any college student who has taken a course in Latin American politics or history during the last 20 years has probably read a book by Petras, Horowitz or Zeitlin.

During the Iran-Iraq war, network news analysis was provided by the same experts who appeared during the recent gulf crisis — Ajami, Kipper and Sick — as well as Johns Hopkins University professors Barry Rubin and Eliott Cohen and Columbia University professor Richard Bulliet. But network reporters and Washington correspondents never interviewed UCLA professor Nikki Keddie, one of this country's leading Iran experts.

When the topic is the Soviet Union or Eastern Europe, reporters invariably turn for analysis to Columbia University professors Zbigniew Brzezinski, Robert Legvold, Jonathan Sanders and Marshall Shulman; Harvard University professor Marshall Goldman; or Princeton University professor Stephen F. Cohen. Reporters also use think tank analysts Dimitri Simes, Ed Hewett, Helmut Sonnenfeldt, and *Foreign Affairs* editor William Hyland as Eastern Europe experts. Before joining the Carnegie Endowment, Brookings Institution and the Council on Foreign Relations, respectively, these three think tank analysts worked at the same private Eastern universities as the other news shapers — Simes and Sonnenfeldt at Johns Hopkins, Hewett and Simes at Columbia, and Hyland at Georgetown after leaving government in 1977. Conspicuously absent among the media's Eastern Europe experts has been Bogdan Denitch, who teaches at the City University of New York and is the author of several books on Yugoslavia and the Cold War. At CUNY, too, Denitch is only blocks away from network studios in midtown Manhattan, closer even than someone from uptown Columbia.

The first month of the gulf crisis network reporters turned to Columbia University professor Edward Said and Georgetown University professors Barry Carter, Michael Hudson and Robert Lieber — in addition to using Sick, Kipper, Ajami and Cordesman. The only notable exception to the beltway group during this period was retired Admiral Crowe, who now teaches at the University of Oklahoma, though it seems doubtful that ABC hired him as a news consultant because of his academic credentials.

Furthermore, few journalists can deny that other journalists seek opinions from the very same experts. The *Boston Globe* reported on December 1, 1987, that "so far this year, [William] Schneider has been quoted more than 300 times in publications tracked by a computer system

— including the *New York Times, Washington Post,* the *Christian Science Monitor,* and the major newsmagazines." Schneider, for the few who do not know, is a Harvard-educated, ex-Harvard professor who is currently a fellow at the American Enterprise Institute and a columnist for the *Los Angeles Times.* Similarly, the *Chronicle of Higher Education* reported in February that "a Nexis computer search for articles that referred to Mr. [Fouad] Ajami or were written by him" turned up 61 listings between August 1990 and mid-January 1991. A DataTimes computer search of 17 newspapers, including the *Los Angeles Times, St. Louis Dispatch, Boston Globe* and *Rocky Mountain News,* revealed that Center for Strategic and International Studies fellow Edward Luttwak was mentioned 78 times between September 1 and December 31, 1990. Luttwak graduated from and taught at Johns Hopkins University before joining the Georgetown-based think tank in 1978.

There is another explanation for the dominance of a few universities in the expert game, and it can be found in reporters' own explanations of the situation. Part of the problem is simple laziness. Sam Donaldson told *Mother Jones* recently that he and other Washington reporters can't take the time to "beat the bushes and launch a search of the city or country" for experts who haven't been seen before. But as thousands of journalists outside of New York and Washington know, it isn't difficult to locate experts. It's a routine followed daily by reporters everywhere. To be fair, many reporters outside the beltway beat are lazy too, and that's why so many universities take the initiative to publicize their people and their work.

So what's going on? In Stephen Hess' sociological study *The Washington Reporters,* recently updated for *Society* magazine, Hess found that Washington reporters tend to be white, male, well educated and from the Northeastern United States. They were very likely to have attended "selective" universities, a likelihood that increased with the prestige of the medium for which they worked. If Hess' research is generalized to how journalists select sources, it stands to reason that reporters go to experts at institutions with which they are familiar.

But there is a special kind of fluidity in this power elite as well. David Gergen leaves government to join a think tank, and after leaving there he can teach at Harvard, then return to government. When his second stint in government has ended, he becomes a journalist and news shaper.

Robin Wright can go from the Carnegie Endowment to the *Los Angeles Times*, and Bernard Trainor can go from the *New York Times* to Harvard.

Examination of the membership and structure of the Council on Foreign Relations, one of the formal institutions that brings think tank analysts, reporters, officials, ex-officials and academics together, reveals the nature and strength of these kinds of institutional bonds. First, the Council is an institution that legitimizes foreign policy expertise, allowing reporters to call upon Council experts without first having to verify their credentials. Second, the Council provides a forum for showcasing its experts; being a speaker at a Council function virtually guarantees that a person will soon thereafter be called as an expert by reporters. Third, the Council is an elite organization that, just as other institutions do, confers status on its members and defines a peer group for them.

The Council was started, and continues to be dominated, by graduates of the more well-known Ivy League universities. One of its founders was Columbia University professor James T. Shotwell, its first secretary was Harvard business school Dean Edwin F. Gay, and the first editor of the Council's journal, *Foreign Affairs*, was Harvard professor Archibald Carey Coolidge. In 1977, 17 percent of Council members had undergraduate degrees from Harvard. Thirteen percent attended Yale, and "if one adds Princeton and Columbia, as well, 48 percent of Council members...attended one of these four universities." The elite composition of the Council is even more dramatic when graduate-level education is considered: Among members with graduate or professional degrees, 70 percent attended Harvard, Yale, Princeton or Columbia.

The Council is just one example of how formal and informal networks in Washington and New York affect the way journalists select their sources from the ranks of academe. In Washington, particularly, journalists are a major component of the beltway establishment. In the March 1990 issue of *Washington Monthly*, veteran reporter James Doyle disparagingly called Washington journalists a "moneyed elite." "Power elite," a term used by sociologists C. Wright Mills and G. William Domhoff, is probably more appropriate. A characteristic of "power elites" is that they maintain contact with other members of the elite, excluding "outsiders." That's what many national media do, and it's one of the reasons so many Americans distrust the news media.

Lawrence C. Soley is an associate professor at the University of Minnesota School of Journalism and contributing editor to *City Pages*.

6

Scholarship in the Public Interest:
Notes from a Soundbite

Richard W. Bulliet

After giving more than 100 news media interviews between August 2, 1991 and the end of the gulf war — for a total of about three minutes of airtime and two column inches of quoted opinion — I have found nothing but confirmation of my long-held view that Middle East crises, and probably crises in general, are like astronomical black holes. The crisis deepens; its gravity increases. As gravity increases, however, certain other things happen.

First, diversity steadily diminishes. Just as the heavier elements, such as plutonium and gold, are broken down and squished until they become nothing but naked quarks, the broad diversity of opinion the news media recruit in the early days of a crisis tends to become more homogeneous as the crisis deepens. A central story line develops, and divergent views are less and less heard.

Second, the deeper you get into a black hole the harder it is for light to escape, until finally no light escapes at all. I do not mean to say that the news media report less and less as a crisis deepens, only that what is reported becomes less and less enlightening. The central story line, all too often dictated by government priorities, becomes so weighty that differing opinions are pushed into the wee hours of the morning or off the air entirely.

Third, the structure of matter progressively breaks down as you are drawn deeper and deeper into a black hole. The media equivalent is identical coverage responding to immediate events drowning out all

61

attempts to look at "the big picture" or the possible future consequences of current action.

My jaundiced view of crisis coverage, of course, is that of a "Middle East expert." In the Persian Gulf crisis, as in previous Middle East crises, the use of regional experts actually diminished as the crisis became more heated. The voices that survived the final influx of "military experts" were few and anodyne compared with the vigorous divergence of opinion that had existed earlier.

In any crisis the ostensible reason for the narrowing of the window for expert opinion is the presence of "hard news." After all, hard news always takes priority over the gabbing of a talking head. In fact, however, genuine hard news was very scarce during the fighting in the gulf because of the controls placed on the news media by the Pentagon. Viewers and readers got to read and hear the same scraps of controlled war information over and over again. Gravity, the desire to share in the great emotional homogeneity of the crisis, was the real culprit.

Now, of course, we have seen the eruption and American abandonment of rebellion in Iraq, the continuation of disorder in Kuwait, the stillbirth of a naive attempt to foster Israeli-Palestinian peace, and the reemergence of Iran as a factor in gulf politics. If these entirely predictable phenomena had been talked about before and during the war, our apparent bewilderment at its anticlimactic aftermath might well have been averted. But, of course, this is what "experts" always say when they feel that what they did not get a chance to say in public might have been of value.

After the Middle East crisis of 1982 I wrote the following advice for a meeting of Middle East scholars, partly to exhort them to their public duty, and partly to make them feel better about the depression evoked by that duty. The advice, and the observations it rests on, is as valid today as it was then.

1. It is okay to talk to the press.

Higher education in general, and Middle East studies as a part of it, is confronted by severe problems: lack of jobs, decreased funding, higher costs, etc. Compounding these problems is a growing lack of interest among the population at large in scholarship outside of the hard sciences. Since ultimately the welfare of scholarship depends upon our society's tacit acceptance of higher education as a societal good worth paying for, the appearance of social utility is worth cultivating, whether or not it is to be regarded as a goal in itself.

Therefore on those occasions when the public, through the media, expresses a desire for expert scholarly opinion, it is in the interest of scholars to respond positively. In other words, despite the fact that the scholar who appears frequently in the press is sometimes viewed by his associates as either a narcissistic panderer or a nincompoop, he or she is actually performing a beneficial publicity service for the entire field.

2. Dealing with the media is dissatisfying.

Encounters with the media are composed half of flattery and half of butchery. The first half requires no explanation; the second arises from editing, quotation out of context, inappropriate juxtaposition with information or opinion from other sources, misinterpretation and so forth. But at a deeper level dissatisfaction with media encounters is psychological. The media interviewer, who is normally no better equipped than a studious undergraduate to understand the details of the matter at hand, acts toward the scholar in the way the scholar likes to act toward his or her students.

The Socratic teacher who asks probing questions, draws forth information and opinion from the student, and then goes on to ask more probing questions is suddenly forced to respond to questions put to him by people he feels are not well qualified to pose them. Typically there is a rush of annoyance that the right question has not been asked. And even when the scholar can pose his or her own questions, an unseen editorial hand cuts and fits the product without regard to the problem carefully built up by the scholar. In short, the scholar, evaluating an experience with a media interviewer, frequently feels that he could have done a better job by himself.

3. The media know their business.

The media are media, that is, they are a middle point between two things: information and the public. Scholars often feel that they are involved in a bilateral relationship with a newspaper or television interviewer, but media people are constantly aware of the mute information consumer as a third party to the transaction. Editorial shaping of questions and responses, therefore, is normally done in light of considerations that journalists feel the scholarly world does not understand or appreciate.

When a scholar cannot express himself or herself rapidly and succinctly in a language devoid of jargon but full of color and inventiveness, the media person tries to turn the encounter into "good air" or "good copy" anyway, or else prestructures the encounter to maximize the likelihood that the outcome will be editorially worthwhile. In this type of situation the scholar frequently feels manipulated before and during the encounter, and distorted in the final product.

Yet it would be a mistake to disregard utterly the existence of the third party. The scholar who carries on an interview as if he were trying to explain things to a slightly deaf and incipiently senile uncle suffers less editorial distortion than the one who imagines that his immediate inter-locutor is his ultimate audience.

4. "The obvious we'll print today; the unusual will take longer."

From their awareness of their public, the media are attuned to discovering the familiar and the expected within the strange and extraordinary. Opinions that stray too far from public expectations are either discarded or interpreted in a normalizing fashion. This is not simply the product of media myopia and simplemindedness; it is rooted in a real perception of the conceptual limits of the ultimate audience and the brevity of its attention.

Nevertheless, insofar as such reductionism leads to an undue favoring of consensus opinions that do not differ from received wisdom and allows the policy agenda of the federal government to set media priorities, this phenomenon should be combated. Experts can only thwart it by making the unfamiliar familiar and understandable, either through frequent repetition or artful presentation. Accurate prediction also does wonders, but even good ideas cannot guarantee accurate prediction.

5. Familiarity ought not breed contempt.

The television network structure of media consulting militates against diversification of opinion. Having one's name in the address book of a reporter or producer is a better guarantee of consultation than actually being expert on the subject at hand. In part this is because a prior consultant has a track record, and reliable, articulate semi-expertise is more valuable to the person facing a deadline than the name of a genuine expert who might be difficult to deal with or have trouble expressing himself in a manner palpable to journalists.

The result is that the same old faces and names recur in the most improbable circumstances. New consultants appear most often when something truly extraordinary happens that clearly requires new types of expertise or, more commonly, that ties up the usual consultants' telephones so badly that new experts are the only recourse.

6. "Give me your opinion, not your advice."

The media usually feel they know what they are doing. News and opinion are their profession, and they do not take kindly to being told their business. The magisterial finger of an unidentified senior editor can often be detected controlling the approach to a story, and no amount of complaint from the consultant can change its course.

The consultant's ability to affect fundamental approaches to a subject is related to his or her track record with the media, but is even more related to the media's confidence in their own grasp of a situation. When, in acknowledgment of a temporary inability to understand what is going on, the media ask for advice rather than opinion, the scholar has a reasonable chance of influencing the shape of the final product. Needless to say, these moments rarely occur.

These views might strike some media professionals as unduly negative and hostile. After all, they are just trying to do their jobs as best they can, and crises put them under particular stress. But experts are people too. Seeing a half-hour interview reduced to a 30-second sound bite or a two-hour consultation with a magazine writer acknowledged by a trivial five-word quote causes pain.

With rare exceptions, your everyday, garden-variety expert receives no remuneration for his or her services, which in a prolonged crisis can add up to several hundred hours of volunteered time. Nor are news organizations or their parent corporations known for giving support to the academic and public service institutions they count on to be there for them in times of need. What would be desirable would be for some "experts" and potential "experts" to get together with some sympathetic media professionals under noncrisis conditions to talk about their relationship. Their common-law marriage could benefit from some wise counseling.

Richard W. Bulliet is professor of history at Columbia University and the former director of its Middle East Institute.

7

Publicize or Perish

Trudi Spigel

In the struggle to survive — if not flourish — in the fierce competition for students, faculty and funding, universities and their public affairs offices are increasingly turning their attention to newspaper op-ed pages. Reputation for most does not rest on centuries of history or legendary athletic teams, and now they must do more than cultivate the downtown daily; they must get the name of the institution and the talents of its faculty into the national press. Hence the invasion of the op-ed market.

In 1984 an op-ed service at Washington University, where I work, was a prospect and a project. It was a next step in the university's national visibility plan, which already included a news feature service and a TV news service to draw attention to the research activities of the faculty. It came, as many things do here, from an imagination of what could be done with the resources at hand. An op-ed service, we dreamed, would add another dimension to this effort. Well-written opinion pieces would bring the university before readers and, in their own way, lift public awareness of the institution.

In particular, we wanted to bring the name and character of the university before readers of national publications such as the *New York Times*, the *Wall Street Journal* and the *Christian Science Monitor*, as well as regional and local journals important to our recruiting and development interests. Our aim was to present Washington firsthand through its experts, as many as possible, junior and senior, across the disciplines and departments. We had only to find those who would grasp the opportunity to reach an audience beyond the classroom. That audience, we were certain, was out there, scattered around the country, in every urban area

67

where there was a major daily with an op-ed page. The experts were at hand, too, throughout the university, a whole population of them with a depth and range of knowledge to give a fresh edge to advocacy and resonance to understanding.

Early in the game I made a set of media calls, with an enlightening if wearing sweep from St. Louis to Portland, Maine — by way of Salt Lake City — then down the coast through Connecticut and back to the Midwest. Almost every editor told me (sometimes kindly) that the university was wasting its time trying to break into the free-lance market. They had their own editorial writers and beyond that subscribed to syndicated services, which they felt obliged to use since they'd already paid for them; torrents of unsolicited material came over the transom daily; they were primarily interested in local issues; academic pieces were too pedantic.

When I asked what the local issues were, local in Dayton, it turned out, was not always so different from local in Denver. Some issues were specific to a community or a region; but many were common to all across the regions. Everyone had concerns that were national and international as well. It was clear that although newspapers and their readers are rooted in communities with pressing local problems, both paper and readers live in a larger world and know it.

Since then I have sent 159 pieces by 62 faculty for 426 placements. Seventeen of Washington's departments or schools are represented in that number, including medicine, law, business, social work, anthropology, political science, history, economics, earth and planetary sciences, physics, education and mathematics. The writers have been scientists, social scientists and humanists, junior faculty and senior faculty, and, in three cases, graduate students; their topics privacy rights, earthquake prediction, defense costs, welfare and social security, the gulf war, lunar research, human rights, the electronic church and more. Pieces have turned up in newspapers in 41 states, with the highest number (outside St. Louis) in Maryland, New Jersey, Florida, Georgia, California and Ohio. That's a telling spread.

There is, to be sure, bashing on both sides. Editors do rail at pompous language, murky arguments, convoluted syntax — as they should. Academics carp at journalists, at editorial pages and editorials. But the fact is that op-ed pages regularly present faculty-written pieces along with essays by experts from think tanks and federal agencies and syndicated columnists. And faculty, though they fume and fulminate, are steady readers of editorial pages.

When I began, I felt the trick would be to know faculty well enough to use them judiciously and effectively — the first trick. The second trick would be to convince them to join the enterprise. The third to make it all work.

To review the faculty and lay a base, I interviewed department chairs. They know their colleagues well; they know what the new research is and what books are under way, where there are deep commitments, abiding interests. They know as well where there's a stubborn tangle of old opinions, where there's been little fresh study. A thorough topical index and complete faculty listing would lay out a heartening view of the range of expertise across the institution. It was, for me, a useful place to start.

At the same time I began a daily discipline of reading, besides the local paper, the national dailies, as well as a range of weekly and monthly magazines and any of the major regional dailies I could get my hands on. I read for issues, for approaches and opinions, and for direct experience with the best in style and argument. I had to know enough about the issues being argued or analyzed to recognize both the egregious and the spurious, to stumble over genuine mistakes in information, and above all to recognize when nothing new was being offered. That meant reading to saturation, and it continues.

I needed an early success — a *New York Times* placement, for example — to give powerful boost to the new service. Every college or university has its important figures. We have ours. They may not always come up with cutting-edge pieces, but they do have visibility — names that editors will recognize. So I began carefully, meeting with faculty who were likely to be recognized, whose expertise gave them a place in current debates, and who might be expected to bring different information and perspective to that debate. I had, to begin with, an economist with an international reputation who had something to say and wanted to say it. His social views bent him to newspaper publication. For him the broader the audience the better. He launched us.

Keeping up with faculty research and publication activity required yet more reading. The serious puff pieces that come out of departments and schools in the course of a year, honest self-congratulation on activity and achievement, are a rich lode of op-ed possibilities. Departmental recruiting materials, which feature their stars, can be mined too. Department meetings, public lectures, symposia, as well as regular meetings with the communication staff of the university public affairs office, all multiplied contacts.

That, though it seems forbidding, is the easy part. Convincing individual faculty to take a hand at writing an opinion piece is another matter. My strategies are simple. I do almost everything face to face. Never letters or memos. Rarely phone calls. I always come to meetings with a potential writer as fully prepared as I can be, knowing what the person's research interests are, with a suggestion for a piece (which I'm prepared to abandon) that might be unique as well as timely. I have guidelines, by design modest and understated; I have my favorite William Safire op-ed and, by now, successful placements from our service artfully selected (writer and newspaper) to bring the candidate into the fold. I lay out the editing process, matters of length, timeliness, placement options, the marketing process.

I make it sound easy: not the writing process, but all the trouble of perfect copies and cover letters and mailing, all the placement efforts. In the beginning these hunting and fishing trips were essential. Now I have, if not a torrent, a steady flow of unsolicited manuscripts.

Editing is, of course, another steeplechase, with different ditches and hedges each time. It's hard for a chaired professor, secure in a tower of successful publication, to take editing suggestions for a newspaper article from an administrator. I can't send out a badly written piece, but the writer may find it hard (or even impossible) to accept change. There are matters of the location of the lead, the clarity of the argument, clouds of unnecessary information, verbs and nouns versus adjectives, weasel words, padding. Every needful change must be negotiated with the writer. Always in person. Always gently. Always clearly, with the specific reason for each one. Firmly. The obstacle course varies with the quality of the first draft and the defenses of the writer. I persist until we are agreed. And I always know, too, that there's another editor out there, at his desk, with a pencil. Some things can be left to that existential reality.

The op-ed piece written and (finally) edited, the question of placement looms. Go for the exclusives? And if so, which one? Send it out on the circuit? In a tight market timeliness is requisite; that may well settle those questions. The competition is ferocious. Some universities and colleges have been bringing their faculty to opinion pages regularly for years.

Stanford, for example, has been very active, as well as Purdue and Penn State. Their media lists range from 200 to less than 50. The enterprise is growing too. A steady stream of university public affairs people have come to me to ask what I do and how.

In our case the mailing list includes 177 newspapers and radio talk shows and stretches from coast to coast, north to south. The list, in its first incarnation, grew out of consultation with admissions and alumni relations officers. Our audience, as we saw it, would be newspaper readers in cities that figured in enrollment and development strategies, wherever admissions and alumni relations wanted to improve visibility. From the beginning that list — one daily in each distribution area — reflected the national spread of the student body.

Over the years I have found other ways to enlarge the circulation of the service and to keep abreast of the needs and interests of editors. I joined the National Conference of Editorial Writers (NCEW), attended their national conventions and sat in on critique sessions. Whatever they said on those ruthlessly intelligent occasions when they went at one another's pages and columns, I took note.

Later I offered conferences for editors on our campus. Designed as in-depth briefing sessions, these affairs brought national and international experts to address the issues and blended our faculty in as discussion participants along with the editors. At one, William Safire and Hodding Carter III joined faculty and editors in a day's discussion of the rhetoric of public discourse. Another time, editors, experts and faculty discussed the global marketplace in a wide-ranging conference that brought to campus high-level representatives from banking (both U.S. and international), Congress, labor, the national defense establishment and industry. It was clear, on each occasion, that the combination of editors and academics made good chemistry.

I try to make our service editor-friendly, to send pieces that will add to the discussion of an issue, pieces that are persuasive, passionate in some way, and fresh; to write a pitch letter that will clue the editor into the gist of the piece quickly and clearly; to send only the best of what I have and that not too often. In a future best-of-all worlds, I'll offer electronic transmission to those who want it, when they want it.

This service has its ups and downs and always will. There's no way to predict which faculty will rise to which issues with what originality or intensity. Beyond that there's no way to guarantee placement of any given piece. It's possible that some editors are lazy, or biased; more likely they are overwhelmed with material, pressed for time, and understaffed. But it is clear that everywhere someone opens the mail and reads it. Rejection forms show that as well as placements. I see not only our faculty in print but those of other colleges and universities. How they came to the op-ed page I don't know.

But they are there. And because they are, connections between the academy and its community — more than ever necessary in a time of growing complexity and ambiguity — are strengthened, and definitions of that community broadened. If the editorial page reflects the conscience of the newspaper, the opinion page, at its best, enlarges and enriches that conscience, bringing the informed judgment of many different thinkers to bear on the great social, political and ethical questions of our age.

Trudi Spigel is director of editorial services at Washington University in St. Louis.

8

College Sports Inc.

Murray Sperber

*We've had 50 players and only three of them
don't have a degree, and we've done that with
freshman eligibility. If we can do it, anybody
can do it.*

—Bob Knight,
Indiana University men's basketball coach,
quoted in the *Bloomington
(Indiana) Herald-Times,*
October 12, 1989

One of the many myths about college basketball is that Bob Knight graduates almost all of his players. The coach proclaims this "fact" and TV commentators and print journalists, including national ones, disseminate it. His fans use the statistic to praise his greatness, and even his enemies admit that he does at least one thing right — he attends to his players' educations.

In reality, of the 72 players to whom Knight has awarded athletic scholarships since he began coaching at Indiana in 1971, only 41 have graduated from the school. In the 1980s his graduation rate was 14 out of 34 recruits, or 42 percent, and, if broken down for black players, two out of 17 — 11 percent. Nevertheless the myth continues, perpetuated by the media.

The amazing aspect of the myth is that Knight's nongraduates were hardly anonymous students. They played basketball in front of huge crowds and were on TV with millions watching. And when they dropped out of school or transferred to other institutions, local and regional media often covered their exits from Indiana in exquisite detail. Yet in a

numbing demonstration of Orwellian doublethink, these same TV stations and newspapers, among them the *Bloomington (Indiana) Herald-
Times*, continue to spread the myth.

But no lie exists forever, and since the publication of Knight's real
graduation statistics in my book, *College Sports Inc.: The Athletic
Department vs. the University*, and the investigations by Tom Witowsky
of the *Des Moines Register* and Ed Sherman of the *Chicago Tribune* into
the rates for all Big 10 schools, Knight has retreated to the claim that
"almost all of my four-year seniors at Indiana have received degrees from
the school." Considering that almost *all* four-year seniors graduate from
their colleges or universities, this is a triumph akin to breathing.

Rather than clean up its act, the *Bloomington (Indiana) Herald-Times*
continues to propagandize for Knight and his basketball program as well
as for other Indiana University varsity teams. "I used to say that reading
the *H-T*'s sports pages was like reading *Pravda*," says one Bloomington
restaurant owner and sports fan. "The *H-T* feeds you the dictator's word,
the party [athletic department] line, and quotes the S.I.D.'s [Sports
Information Director's] propaganda as straight news. But I can't use that
analogy anymore — *Pravda* has loosened up."

If college sports were just fun and games and American higher
education were wonderfully rich and could afford all kinds of divertisse-
ments, then the media coverage of intercollegiate athletics would not be
an issue. In college sports today, however, with increasing tension
between big-time athletic departments and the universities that house
them, and the accelerating attempts by various groups, especially college
presidents and faculty, to solve the systemic problems afflicting intercollegiate athletics, the media play a crucial role in forming and mobilizing
public opinion. Unfortunately, because of the media's "special interest
network" with athletic department personnel, they are usually on the side
of the college sports establishment and against reform.

The public, however, assumes that media coverage of the reformers
and their agenda is honest and unbiased. In fact, a whole world of
subjectivity and conflict of interest lies beneath the texts on the sports
pages and the phrases and images on radio and TV. Sometimes this media
bias is conscious, but usually it originates in ignorance and unconscious
prejudice. Whatever its source, the result is that too often the media
propagandize for athletic department interests and attack those in higher

education who are trying to bring college sports into line with academic goals.

> *Whenever I go on campus to cover a game, I try*
> *to see some of the academic parts of the school.*
> *I'm about the only person in the press box to do*
> *that.*
> —William C. Rhodden, *New York Times*

With a few exceptions, most sports editors and reporters are badly informed about the educational operations and missions of the schools whose teams they cover. They were only inside higher education during their undergraduate years and, like almost all undergrads, they gained very little understanding of a university's inner workings or even its purposes. Later, as sports journalists, when they come to cover athletic events and stories they rarely venture beyond the stadiums and arenas and almost never talk to people outside the athletic department.

Sports editors and reporters also develop an unhealthy dependency upon athletic department personnel and press releases and are very unwilling to criticize these sources or their point of view. The local press frequently reprints publicity pablum as authentic news; regional and national media are more adept at changing noun and verb constructions, but they rarely question the content — or lack of same — of the handouts. In addition, the media always go along with the athletic department's euphemism for its publicity office, obediently calling it the "sports information department," referring to the head flak by his or her chosen title, usually "sports information director," and subordinates as "assistant SIDs," etc. (The media never do this when covering professional sports — there are no "information directors" for pro teams, only publicity people.)

This coziness with athletic department publicists carries over into sports journalists' desire to please the coaches and athletes. Sometimes this relationship is conscious: Bob Hammel, sports editor of the *Bloomington (Indiana) Herald-Times*, is one of Bob Knight's best friends, and many other sports reporters become personally friendly with coaches and, to a lesser extent, with athletes, and thus try to give them favorable coverage. But even those reporters who are not close to the coaches and athletes have a problem because the athletic department expects them to be cheerleaders for the college teams — not objective journalists reporting on the complexities, personalities and issues in college sports.

The nature of sports itself — its deceptive simplicity — is partly responsible for the cheerleader problem. In our world of complication and disarray, the fact that a game and a season are clearly won or lost is attractive to most sports fans and participants. Coaches and athletes particularly see the world in simple, clear terms — they won or they lost and the final score announces it for all to see. As a result, most coaches and athletes expect the media to portray them in equally simple terms — you're for us 100 percent or you're against us. There is no in-between, no gray area, no shade and nuance.

In my years of sports reporting, I never met a coach, an athlete or an athletic administrator who acknowledged that an issue had more than two sides — the home side and the opposition — or that some truths might exist below, above, or in between the two poles. When athletic department people deal with the press, they bring this Manichean world view with them and they cannot understand journalists who want to investigate finances or conflicts of interest or anything beyond the preparation for and action on the field or court. In their eyes, any journalist who strays from the cheerleader stance, even into mild nuance, becomes an untrustworthy opponent.

Bob Knight is the most famous basketball coach of this generation and a role model for many of his peers. In the late 1970s, a student writer on the *Indiana [University] Daily Student* criticized Knight in print. Since then the coach has refused to grant an interview to any *Daily* reporter — although the offender left the University long ago and no one, possibly not even Knight, can remember the offending item. For Knight, *Daily* staffers — past, present and future — have joined his lengthy list of enemies, apparently never to be removed. (This situation is also interesting because the media frequently refer to Knight as "a great teacher" but have never reported his refusal to cooperate in the education of I.U. student journalists. One assumes that beat reporters avoid this story because they fear incurring this coach's famous wrath and being sent to a similar "Coventry.")

In addition to the psychological bribery that coaches and athletic directors use by favoring those reporters who "are on the team" and excluding "troublemakers," athletic departments use a more direct form of bribery. Many beat reporters assigned to a college squad travel to away games on the team's charter plane, have their hotel and food expenses picked up by the athletic department, and are included in the lavish weeks for football bowl games and NCAA tournaments. In addition, if they work for morning papers, the team will often delay the postgame departure of the charter flight so that the reporters can file their stories. These same reporters usually deny that any conflict of interest exists or that their ongoing stream of favorable articles on the college team, coach and players has anything to do with these privileges and gifts.

Conversely, if a beat reporter writes even the mildest criticism of a coach, athlete or some aspect of an athletic program — no matter how true and accurate the comment — the reporter often has to make private arrangements to cover away games, at his or her employer's expense.

Well so what, you say.

All of the problems of the media covering college sports would be sideshow and unimportant if they did not affect the coverage of major areas of conflict between athletic departments and their host universities, especially the current disputes about the financing of college sports. If a simple myth like Bob Knight's graduation rates took so long to debunk — and all anybody had to do was take a list of Knight's players to the registrar of Indiana University and ask whether they received their degrees or not — what about the more complex and important myths that encrust college sports? An examination of a crucial one — money — and how and why the press has not investigated it, provides a case study for the entire issue.

> You can probably count on your two hands the
> number of athletic departments that actually
> have a surplus annually.
> —Dick Schultz, executive director of the NCAA

One of the best-kept secrets about intercollegiate athletics — well guarded because athletic departments are extremely reluctant to open their financial books — is that in spite of the huge amount of revenue from ticket sales and TV rights fees, most athletic departments lose money. If profit-and-loss is defined according to ordinary business practices, of the 803 members of the NCAA, the 493 of the NAIA, and the more than 1,050 junior colleges, only 10 to 20 athletic programs make a consistent, albeit small, profit, and in any given year, another 20 to 30 break even or come close. All of the rest — more than 2,300 — lose anywhere from a few dollars to millions annually on college sports.

Even the NCAA acknowledges the poor financial health of college sports. Its most recent study on this topic, *The Revenues and Expenses of Intercollegiate Athletic Programs*, polled member athletic departments and reported that the vast majority lost money. For example, in 1988-89 the University of Michigan's athletic program — in spite of a consistently sold-out 101,700-seat stadium *and* victories in the Rose Bowl *and* in the NCAA men's basketball tournament *and* earnings of $3.5 million from these events — ended the year $2.5 million in the red and projected a $5.3 million annual deficit for the early 1990s.

The myth that college sports are immensely profitable for the *schools* that supply the teams is simply not true, and the corollary — that the money earned from this enterprise helps other parts of the university — is also false. All of the revenue that athletic departments generate stays in their cash drawer and, at the end of the year, when the drawer is empty, they *take* money from other parts of their colleges and universities, usually from the General Operating Fund. In other words, dollars that could go for educational purposes disappear down the college sports deficit hole. Don Tyson, Chairman of Tyson Foods and a member of the State of Arkansas Higher Education Committee, put the matter succinctly when he commented on the multimillion-dollar athletic department deficits in his state: "We've got the deal spotted. If they [athletic departments] don't get enough money, they steal it out of the education budget."

> *When I went after athletic department books at public universities, even though I clearly had the state freedom of information laws on my side, it was always me and my lawyer and very shallow pockets, against the athletic department and the university's lawyers and very deep pockets. I was told by one school that they would fight me to the state supreme court rather than open their athletic department's books.*
> —A personal anecdote related to Bill Moyers on the PBS special "Sports for Sale"

Ascertaining the exact amount of red ink in college sports is extremely difficult. Because athletic departments are often autonomous or semiautonomous units with little real supervision by university officials, they can erect "Iron Curtains" around their operations. Even at public universities, where no legal justification exists for their secrecy, they will not reveal their true financial situation. Only the most tenacious newspaper reporters and academics have been willing to search for the facts, and only those newspapers such as *USA Today*, which can afford and has been willing to meet the legal costs, have been consistently successful. (In 1986, *USA Today* did a very comprehensive survey of college football and basketball coaches' salaries, perks, deals and financial scams, and single-handedly set in motion a number of academic studies of this problem.)

In addition, because athletic departments use "creative accounting" methods to remove as many expenses as possible from their books, they are adept at concealing millions of dollars of losses. Their real annual deficits are much more extensive than the NCAA and individual athletic directors admit, and reading their financial books requires an expertise that most investigators lack.

Nonetheless, if a reporter is serious about examining athletic department finances, the first item to study is the most obvious and the most overlooked: the immediately visible symbols of college sports — its huge stadiums and arenas. Ironically, the most significant hidden cost in intercollegiate athletics is the financing and maintenance of these facilities. Very few schools build a stadium or an arena with cash up front; they borrow the money instead, and thereafter someone has to pay the interest charges and try to retire the debt. That someone is usually the students, who finance the deal in the form of mandatory annual fees. At most state of Virginia schools, for example, each student pays at least $100 a year — often placed in the innocuous appearing "activity fees" item on the student's bill — for debt-servicing and other athletic department expenses. In most cases the students are unaware that they are paying part of the athletic department's bills by means of this hidden tax.

Moreover because of what sociologist Harry Edwards terms the "athletic arms race," coaches and athletic directors demand state-of-the-art facilities and can never stop spending to acquire them. In the last decade, almost all Big 10 athletic departments built multimillion-dollar indoor football practice fields at the same time that the legislatures in these rust-belt states were cutting funding to higher education.

Once the stadiums and other facilities are built, maintaining them is enormously expensive. Football stadiums, used five or six times a year, need special care because of the stress on concrete during cold winters and hot summers. Indoor arenas, weightrooms, et al. are also costly to maintain, and whenever possible, athletic departments move these maintenance costs off their books and into the "buildings-and-grounds" line in the university budget. Some athletic departments then claim that they have balanced their books, and reporters dutifully report this "fact." If the press would probe these claims and examine the maintenance and debt-servicing expenses of athletic departments, the reality would amaze them and their readers.

The single greatest expense for athletic programs, however, is personnel. This year, most big-time athletic departments will pay more than $5 million in wages and benefits to their employees (athletic departments are notorious for their bloated payrolls and nepotism). Schools often absorb a large part of this expense by placing athletic program personnel, including coaches, on regular faculty or staff lines in their budgets, even though few of these people see the inside of a classroom on a regular basis or do any work for the university other than college sports tasks. At state institutions, personnel lines in the budget are public information and schools have to reveal them (often the library reference desk keeps the master list). A reporter armed with a list of an athletic department's coaches and staff — instantly obtained from the department's publicity office — can easily discover their salaries as well as whether they are listed as teaching personnel.

Another multimillion-dollar item often removed from athletic department books is the expense for so-called grants-in-aid, otherwise known as athletic scholarships. Athletes are the only group of students recruited for commercial entertainment, not academic purposes, and they are the only students who go through school on grants based on their talent and potential as commercial entertainers, not on their educational aptitude. Nevertheless, the NCAA admits that many athletic departments "that award grant-in-aid to participating athletes do not report these costs as operating expenses" because they are able to get their schools to fund them out of regular student scholarship money or other sources. This financial maneuver becomes particularly pernicious when institutions allow coaches to take Opportunity Grant and other money targeted for needy minority students and award it instead to athletes with minimal SAT scores and little aptitude for or interest in college work.

Another neat grant-in-aid trick is the "out-of-state/in-state" shell game. At public institutions, some athletic departments pay tuition for out-of-state athletes at in-state rates, reducing their expense by six-figure amounts. Reporters could take the game programs, ascertain the athletes' hometowns, and then ask the university to supply copies of the fee statements for these athletes.

The NCAA also admits that a majority of athletic departments receive "direct state or other government support" and that at many public institutions with big-time programs this comes to over $1 million a year. When he was athletic director at the University of Virginia, Dick Schultz told the *Richmond Times Dispatch* that "A five- to six-million dollar program ought to be able to generate its own revenue without resorting to public funds. Taking state tax money places you in a position of people being able to say you're taking money that could be used for general education." Schultz added, "I know public money is tempting but I like to be able to look professors in the eye." Now that he has become executive director of the NCAA, Schultz has yet to convince the college sports establishment of his position on this issue.

The NCAA acknowledges that "direct" government subsidies help support intercollegiate athletics. In fact, athletic departments at both public and private colleges receive millions more in *indirect* subsidies. In the rulings on Temple University's challenge to Title IX, the courts pointed out that Temple's athletic program "benefits from governmental aid to other branches of the university. Federal money to those other branches allows the university to divert other funds to the sports program." Divert seems too mild a verb for what can occur in the various money-laundering schemes used by some athletic programs and compliant university officials.

In similar ways, central administrators cover a huge number of miscellaneous athletic department expenses or pass on those costs to the students: The pharmacy department or the university health service assumes the increasingly expensive drug tests mandated by the NCAA; some of the medical personnel who service the intercollegiate athletes are paid out of health service funds; the athletic department's legal problems are taken care of by the university attorney's office; the telephone bill for recruiting (often a $50,000-plus item) is moved to the university-wide telephone bill; and every other possible expense that an athletic director can convince a central administrator to carry vanishes from the AD's books. If reporters would inquire into these financial maneuvers and inform the people paying these bills — the taxpayers as well as students and their parents — much of this subterfuge might end.

*Despite the pious half-time pronouncements we
see on televised football and basketball games, in
which the future of humankind is tied to the missions of universities with big-time athletic
programs, these very programs contradict the
fundamental aims of American higher education.*
—Richard Warch,
president of Lawrence University,
Appleton, Wisconsin

Because the commercial objectives and operating methods of College
Sports Inc. are totally separate from and mainly opposed to the educational aims of the institutions that house its franchises, the justifications
for big-time college sports are increasingly shaky. Moreover, the many
tricks and devices that athletic departments use to underwrite their annual
deficits prompt questions about their continuing existence. In an era
when the academic units of most colleges and universities go begging
for money, when classroom buildings and research labs are falling apart,
when tuition and other student costs are rising exponentially, when
graduate teaching assistants are not paid a living wage nor faculty
commensurate with their professional skills, does it make sense to feed
the athletic department deficit?

In the 1990s, because of the increasingly expensive athletics arms race
and in spite of the infusion of TV dollars into the NCAA, these deficits
will increase. College sports is undergoing systemic failure and only
major surgery can save the patient.

The best ally for the reform movement is an honest and active press.
National magazines and newspapers, and even a few local ones like the
Lexington (Kentucky) Herald-Leader, have exposed some of the recruiting and booster scandals involving various athletes, coaches and athletic
departments. But recruiting and booster scandals are a result of the
systemic problems in college sports, not the cause. Editors must now
assign reporters to investigate the less sexy issue of the finances of
athletic departments and expose this root problem. Probably special task
forces will be more effective than beat reporters because task force
journalists are not beholden to athletic department personnel. In this way
the media can short-circuit the "special interest network" and even
expose the ways in which the network's "goals [are] quite different" and
generally opposed to "the stated purpose of the university."

William Atchley, former president of Clemson University and now head of the University of the Pacific, and an administrator with long experience on these issues, summed up the tension between College Sports Inc. and American higher education: "When academics take a back seat to athletics, you have a problem. You no longer have an institution where people with integrity want to teach, or where people with common sense and good values want to send their children to learn."

Unless American higher education solves this problem, College Sports Inc. will continue to corrupt it, and with increasing speed. The reformers want to derail the athletic department juggernaut. The press should report on this conflict as honestly and fairly as possible instead of riding in the club car of the athletic department's high-speed train.

Murray Sperber is an associate professor of English and American Studies at Indiana University, Bloomington.

PART II

Journalism in the University

9

Grub Street in the Groves of Academe

Ceil Cleveland

In October 1977, when I arrived at Columbia University looking for work, I had already taught in the English departments of three universities, written for two major newspapers and edited four books. With a partner and a couple of grants, I had also established a literary press that had published six volumes of fiction and poetry by women.

I saw myself then, as I do today, as equal parts teacher and writer. In 1977 I was not sure whether it was the Year of the Teacher or the Year of the Writer. Through a happy and quite unforeseen circumstance, it turned out to be both.

When I delivered myself to the steps of Low Library, I was pointed in the direction of a new vice president who, rumble had it, was looking for someone to edit a new (undefined) magazine for a new (undefined) purpose. I convinced the man to let me take it on and was hired virtually on the spot as editor in chief (I made up my title, since no one knew what to call me) of a nonexistent publication. Just as promptly, I was assigned to a dank office with a good address (the Journalism Building) and a nonfunctioning typewriter. Then I was left entirely alone.

The best part was the last. I approached my existential task with a quotation from Pascal, "The eternal silence of these infinite spaces frightens me," tacked to my peeling wall. Suffering the exquisite anguish of benign neglect, I set out to create a magazine.

No policy was in place to govern what I was supposed to do, nor were there any stated objectives. In a bureaucracy, asking permission almost always elicits a "No." So I never asked: "Am I in charge here? Do I have the final say? Is this a job for a real journalist?"

I figured that if I used my intuition, and got it right, I'd add a spark of creativity to the environment; if I got it wrong, they could fire me. Both struck me as preferable to having someone look over my shoulder. I realized that if I demanded objectives, I was likely to be told to produce an "alumni" publication, and all the impressions I had about "alumni" publications were negative.

Over the years I had seen an awful lot of stuff dispatched from universities to alumni — for the most part, dull, poorly written tabloids, or glossy newsletters, filled with fund-raising appeals and items about promotions, new babies, and blissful holidays in Maui. This material was illustrated by fuzzy grip-and-grin photos, 20 bodies clustered together in one murky photographic blob and banal clip art. To my mind, this had nothing to do with education.

But here I was, by default, with *carte blanche*. So what was I to do with this *tabula rasa*? I sat down and made a short list. I wanted:

a. to conceive and edit a magazine that I would like to read.

b. to create a publication that took up where higher education in a classroom left off, one that not so much contained "news" as dealt with the ideas behind the news.

c. to uncover the interesting work that was going on in university classrooms, departments, labs and research centers and translate it for a highly educated but general audience.

d. to treat a large university campus as a journalist would treat a small city, covering it like a beat.

I wanted to create what I began to think of as "a university magazine" — a general-interest publication that passed the "dentist's office test" (i.e., if you picked it up there, would you read it?).

I asked for printouts of all faculty and alumni (at that time about 90,000), and when I ran across a name of someone whose work I knew, I called. I needed writers, ideas, advice. I got it. From Asimov to Zbigniew, people responded.

The following spring I published a magazine. Hardly anyone on campus noticed (though it was mailed to thousands of alumni across the country), and for the abject anonymity I was grateful. It was not that the magazine was bad; it contained some provocative articles ("De-Institutionalization, A Vastly Oversold Good Idea," by sociologist Amitai Etzioni, and "Will Green Plants Replace Oil?"), but it was a jumble. Nine years later, when I left the editorship, *Columbia* — a university magazine

— had won more awards than we had wall space for and been honored by the Council for Advancement and Support of Education (CASE) as a Magazine of the Decade.

Early in my editorship, while I was studiously reinventing the wheel, I discovered that not all alumni magazines were drab, unreadable things, and that other university editors — at Brown, Johns Hopkins, the University of Pennsylvania, Harvard, Notre Dame — were already producing the kind of magazine I envisioned. (Indeed, Columbia itself had produced one of the best in the 1960s.) A few of these journalists, it turned out, had been working on an improvement of the breed since 1957.

Their experiments had led not only to the elevation of alumni publications across the country, but to the creation of the *Chronicle of Higher Education*, which has become to higher education what the *Wall Street Journal* is to business. Led by Corbin Gwaltney (now editor of the *Chronicle*), who a few years earlier had transformed *Johns Hopkins Magazine* from a dreary rag to a model of photojournalism, a group of 15 alumni magazine editors consulted a prominent editor at *The Saturday Evening Post* for advice. According to one of them, Ron Wolk, the group was told: "You guys are doing a nice job, but you're speaking only to your own alumni. What would happen if you spoke about education with one voice to the world in general?"

This comment spurred the group (which included Robert M. Rhodes, now editor of *Brown Alumni Monthly*) to commit a portion of their budgets — bulwarked by a grant from the Carnegie Corporation of New York — to create one stunning 32-page report, *American Higher Education: 1958*. In this era of Sputnik, they decided to call it a "Moonshooter." As an afterthought, they offered the report to other institutions; 150 universities paid a nickel a copy and bound it into their alumni publications.

So successful was the project that Carnegie gave the group a second grant, with which they founded Editorial Projects in Education. For the next 22 years, EPE published reports annually on various issues in higher education for binding into alumni magazines. At its peak the report reached 3 million alumni of more than 300 institutions. The group also launched *The 15 Minute Report*, a Kiplinger-style newsletter for university trustees, and began syndicating news and feature articles to alumni magazines.

The enterprising journalists, however, were not finished: Gwaltney and Wolk sold their dream of creating a national weekly newspaper to Carnegie. With a grant of $120,000, the *Chronicle* was born in 1966. A few times it was on the verge of bankruptcy, and then boomtime hit: "There's no question that affirmative action made us grow," says Gwaltney. When colleges and universities found that they were required, by law, to advertise for positions, the *Chronicle* was the logical place.

Now owned by Gwaltney and publisher John Crowl, the *Chronicle* has grown in 25 years to include 60 pages of ads, and has a circulation of 92,000 and a staff of 140. Taking charge of EPE, Wolk developed a new publication to serve elementary and secondary education, *Education Week*, and two years ago created *Teacher* for secondary-school teachers.

As the Moonshooters were being launched, George Keller, at Columbia, was setting off his own rockets. Says Wolk: "We had moved education writing, alumni publishing, out of the chatty, check-handing, class-notes stuff into thoughtful issue-oriented pieces. But Keller, in the '60s, challenged the educational institution itself." This, as it happened, was rather like an editor at *Time* picking a fight with Henry Luce.

Between 1963 and 1969, Keller, a former English professor and dean, edited a quarterly called *Columbia College Today*. "What I had in mind at the time was a very novel idea," says Keller now. "I wondered, could you really report honestly without getting into hot water? Could you report from the inside, as if you were a journalist on the outside?"

Keller took some tough positions: "Questioning some practices of fraternities got me in some trouble. And some people didn't like it when I wrote that an architect was messing up the McKim Mead White architectural concept on campus, putting up grisly buildings and not even consulting the School of Architecture, which was very good." The hot water rose above Keller's ankles.

Then came the revolution. Says Keller: "The climate on the campuses in the late '60s demanded a change in reporting; no longer could any editor get away with doing puff stuff. How could you write pap to your alumni when they could see on the nightly news that campuses were exploding all over the country?" In the spring of 1968, Keller dedicated an entire issue to an analysis and on-the-spot issue he wrote himself. Almost book-length, "Six Weeks That Shook Morningside" won the highest awards in academic publishing and was seen as seminal in educational journalism.

But the hot water steamed. Keller's frankness shocked and angered some university officials. It so aroused the ire of radical students that the lives of his wife and small children were threatened. "It was a really mean time," Keller says. "The radical Ted Gold, who later blew himself up, threatened to blow up my home on 103rd Street. So it was time for me to move upstate and edit a research magazine for SUNY." For nearly a decade thereafter, Columbia had no magazine of record.

Though he admits writing "with candor," Keller (who now chairs the division of higher education at the University of Pennsylvania's Graduate School of Education) insists he "always wrote with affection for the institution." Education, he says, needs journalists who "really care, but who know what's going on — who have an in-depth knowledge. In news land, education is a dog beat. Those of us who think it's interesting tend to be in universities. Nobody else is writing well or thoughtfully about education, so a good alumni magazine is a lemonade stand in the desert."

It is true that little thoughtful, comprehensive education writing can be found elsewhere. Most newspapers and magazines don't have education editors, and on television only the public network gives the subject more than cursory coverage. "Newspaper writers get excited about education only when there are sports, rapes, dope and budget scandals on campus," Keller says. "They don't understand the curricular stuff, which is complex; and when that's covered at all it tends to be done in magazines."

Journalists may have a bad rep in some quarters, but many alumni magazine editors identify themselves as such. I questioned 12 of the country's best (as recognized by CASE during the past several years). Five call themselves journalists; six, editors; and one, a public-relations professional (this one having become "more cynical, but not totally jaded").

When asked whose work they most admired, they tended to name each others' — with Walton Collins, editor of *Notre Dame Magazine*, cited most often. (In Boston, where the Cabots speak only to the Lodges, John Bethell, editor of *Harvard Magazine*, cites only I.F. Stone.) Two have journalism degrees and one a Ph.D. in English. Surprisingly, only two received degrees from the institutions they now represent to their alumni.

All but one of these editors have worked in print journalism — most in responsible positions on dailies — yet some bad blood exists between journalists inside and outside educational institutions. Though nine of the

12 claimed editorial autonomy and said they edit from their own points of view, rather than the administration's, the question that brought the most heated replies from university editors was this: "Have you ever felt devalued because you are not a 'real journalist' or a 'real reporter' — meaning that you work inside an educational institution rather than report its doings from the outside?"

Elise Hancock, who has applied her considerable creative talents to editing *Johns Hopkins Magazine* for 18 years, replies: "Not among people I respect. [They] tend to look at my work before deciding [whether] it's 'only' an alumni magazine. Inside the institution, . . . a culture in which 'seeking publicity' is considered a low-class thing to do, 'real reporters' are despised. The 'real' press has bitten these people all too often, notably promising 'cures' when something was just preliminary research and not even yet in clinical trials."

Says John Bethell of *Harvard Magazine*: "No. The opposite. Because so much of the reporting coming from outside is superficial, ill founded or inaccurate."

John Soisson of the University of Portland disagrees: "Yes, I think there is a general view — both inside and outside the academy — that our work is not true journalism because we are advocates paid by the university."

Meg Dooley (who followed me at *Columbia*) comments: "Yes and no. In the company of 'real' journalists I sometimes feel that way, but at other times the behavior of 'real' journalists seems so irresponsible to me that I'm thankful I'm not one of them."

Stephen Lyons of the University of Idaho, who set off a heated exchange with a recent *Chronicle* essay arguing that alumni magazine editors should be journalists first and promoters of their institution only secondarily, reports: "My director tells us all the time that we are not 'real journalists.' That hurts. What are we then?"

Marshall Ledger, a scholar of English literature and editor of *Penn Medicine*, says that once at an academic conference a *St. Louis Post-Dispatch* reporter, who did not know either Ledger or his magazine, dismissed both as simply institutional tools. "I felt so devalued, let me tell you, that I have never forgotten it," Ledger recalls. "I've mulled it over. . . . I examine the work of 'real' journalists to see just how free from or slavish to pressures they are. I notice, for instance, that the sports pages are virtually free ads, yet they parade as 'objective' or whatever. I notice that, in the early days of the Persian Gulf war, it was virtually impossible to find, on the level of the *Post-Dispatch*, skeptical or questioning reporters, let alone any dissenting ones."

Robert L. Bliwise, editor of *Duke University Magazine*, says he doesn't consider his work devalued "because I work for a university; I do consider it shaped by that association. But the direction of any editorial product, it seems to me, is shaped by the interests and the mission of the publisher — whether the publisher is, say, a national newspaper or a university. . . . I also think it's important for an editor to believe in the mission of his publisher; and it seems to me an easy thing to believe in the mission of higher education."

Most of the university editors admitted that their magazines, as Ledger put it, "do have grave limitations as news sources." But a few, like Bethell of Harvard and Collins of Notre Dame, have carried "breaking news" stories, picked up by national broadcast and print media. Duke's Bliwise, on the other hand, notes that "spotting trends, not breaking news," is important to him. Shortly after his magazine profiled a controversial professor in the "hot" Duke English department, the professor became a major feature in the *New York Times Magazine*.

But Ledger is on to something. Though academic journalists are frequently irritated with the shallowness of the research of those who report from the outside, we may be faulted not for caving into institutional pressures so much as for our own parochial points of view. We don't break our necks to find a dissenting voice as counterpoint when we announce that "our" scientist has come up with a stunning "break-through," and we don't often carry negative reviews of "our" faculty's books — though it's been known to happen.

Grub Street does meet Academe, as Nona Balakian, an editor of the *New York Times Book Review*, once wrote in *Columbia*. An alumni magazine is where "specialized knowledge" is combined "with the newspaperman's skill in reaching a public that reads on the run." Surely it is an awareness of this intersection that frequently leads newspaper and magazine editors to reprint alumni magazine articles. Examples: the *Washington Post* and *Reader's Digest* (Harvard), *The Chicago Tribune* and *Family Living* (Notre Dame), *Esquire* and *Science Digest* (Columbia). Bantam Books picked up an entire series on health developed by Laura Freid, then editor of Boston University's *Bostonia*.

But I must acknowledge that these are illustrations of alumni publishing at its best. These editors have an extraordinary amount of editorial autonomy. Yet even they can pour out anecdotes, ranging from humiliating to hilarious, about the times their work has gotten them in trouble with faculty and administrators. And the great majority of alumni editors — those whose work does not show up year after year on the roster of top 10 magazines — are on much shorter chokes.

The evidence, both anecdotal and analytical, indicates that the editor is the critical factor. A 1985 University of Michigan study ("Alumni Periodicals: The Forgotten Genre," by Leslie B. Levine) concluded that "the single most important variable in determining the success of an alumni periodical is the editor, and this is independent of all other variables." Yet even the strongest editor cannot create and maintain a successful (meaning well-read, credible and respected) magazine without support from the highest institutional sources, from the president on down. As one university editor put it, "You're only as good as your boss will allow you to be."

It is certainly clear to me that without the hands-off attitudes of my immediate bosses over the years, *Columbia* would never have been created, nor could it ever have matured into a respected publication without presidential support.

A perennially volatile issue for editors is the relationship between fund raising and their magazines. In a 1988 survey conducted at the University of Maryland, Donna Shoemaker asked a nationwide sampling of 900 campus editors, alumni professionals and journalism educators: How important is "focusing on fund-raising news in alumni periodicals"? Only 6 percent of campus editors saw this goal as "very important," compared with 18 percent of alumni relations professionals. This is not surprising; what is startling, if not downright ironic, is that 24 percent of journalism educators said fund-raising news was a "very important" goal for an alumni periodical!

It's clear that alumni magazine journalists are serious about what they do and consider theirs a profession; most remain in their jobs for years, though all of them believe they could make more money plying the same skills outside academia. (John Marcham has been in his post at Cornell for 28 years, and Bethell in his at Harvard for 25.) Most see themselves in privileged positions, and why wouldn't they? Their beats contain the most brilliant minds and the most exciting research in the world. And their readers are the best educated, if also the most demanding — as editors quickly learn from their letters should they misspell the name of a fourteenth-century Central European prince.

Certainly the scope and depth of the better alumni publications are comparable to the better commercial magazines and serious newspapers. Here's a sampling of university magazine articles for the year 1989:

- A study of women in the Third Reich and of a presumed "gender response" to evil (Duke);

- The work of a pediatric neurosurgeon who emerged from inner-city poverty to treat the fragile brains of children (Johns Hopkins);

- An investigation into our national obsession with weight loss; and a measure of racial tensions on campus (Brown);

- Examination by CalTech scientists of the "discovery" of cold fusion (*Engineering and Science*);

- A profile of the work of the first network TV news anchor, Douglas Edwards (Emory);

- The interaction of undergraduate writers with Pulitzer Prize-winning poet W.S. Merwin (*Pennsylvania Gazette*);

- An examination of whether coal can clean up its act and become America's energy choice once again (*Pitt Magazine*);

- In "Why Johnny Kills," a physician's psychiatric portrait of violent juveniles and adults (*NYU Magazine*).

The work of alumni editors may not be as glamorous or sexy as that in magazines that deal with fashion, entertainment, celebrity lifestyles and home decorating. But the worlds of art, music, dance, theater, travel, books, health, science, economics, international affairs, law, business, and social and cultural issues are wide open to the academic journalist. Editors in these settings know their sources and have instant access. And since most magazines are on cycles that range from quarterly to monthly, academic journalists have — and take — time to check their facts before they go to press.

No alumni magazine can compete with *People*, *McCall's* or *GQ*. But then, why would it want to? The beat of the journalist in academe is that of a different drummer. These editors can allow mind and imagination to soar — so long as, of course, they keep a firm grip on the obvious and announce it from time to time.

Ceil Cleveland, founding editor of *Columbia, The Magazine of Columbia University*, is communications consultant to many colleges and universities, writes regularly for consumer magazines, and is author of *In the World of Literature*.

10

The Best Campus Dailies

Jacki Hampton

It's a dirty job selecting the top college newspapers in the country, but someone's got to do it. At *U. The National College Newspaper*, ink blackens our fingers as we read the more than 400 college papers sent to us by members of the American Collegiate Network, representing college publications from every state. We comb the papers each day, looking for the best stories, photographs and illustrations to fill the pages of *U.*, our monthly national newspaper.

In the years since *U.*'s first issue, several student papers have earned reputations — some not so enviable — for different aspects of their publications. There are those, like the *Daily Nebraskan*, that we rely on for up-to-date, well-written album reviews and entertainment news. Others, like the *Daily Iowan*, always provide strong color feature photos. Some simply provide a good laugh every now and then, such as the papers that run well-meaning but ridiculous headlines: "Student plummets down credit card vortex" and "She's from Africa, Kenya believe it?"

In a market where editors balance daily deadlines with term papers and exams, writers are either underpaid or not paid at all, and papers are often funded by the very administrations they're trying to "watchdog," it's not easy to produce a consistently solid news product. The campus newspaper must serve the specific needs of its audience, informing about campus events for every group and faction, yet resisting the urge to become simply an expanded calendar. Staff members must fairly and accurately present issues that directly affect them as students while not becoming a public relations tool. Finally, the paper must maintain a professional image while allowing freedom for experimentation and learning by student journalists.

In addition, there are strengths and weaknesses that may not be readily apparent to the average reader of any given paper but which stand out to *U.* editors as we read it alongside 400 others. Certain characteristics — which include original, risk-taking designs, local stories with the extra punch and validity gained by researching their national relevance, and other above-and-beyond-the-call-of-duty qualities — separate a few outstanding papers from other very adequate publications. With these requisites in mind, the editorial staff at *U.* undertook the task of listing the 15 best campus newspapers we have seen.

This list is limited to daily newspapers; we believe the student staffs meeting daily and still producing consistently strong material deserve special attention. Several of these campus papers face the extra responsibility of serving as the community paper. *The Daily Californian*, for example, is the only daily paper in Berkeley, a city of more than 100,000. The University of North Carolina's *Daily Tar Heel* has the largest circulation of any newspaper, professional or student, in the county — including, for example, the *Raleigh News & Observer* — and it is distributed in three additional counties as well. These papers must strike a balance between campus and city coverage.

Before naming the best that we've seen, I want to clarify that a paper's inclusion — or exclusion — does not necessarily reflect on the journalism program at that school. In fact, some of the schools included do not even offer journalism degrees, a fact that makes their students' accomplishments even more impressive. And some schools with extremely good preparatory programs simply do not have the funding to produce a daily, high-quality printed product.

The papers we have found to be consistently strong, come "back to school" or midterm, campus outbreak of measles or national outbreak of war, are, in alphabetical order:

Daily Bruin, University of California, Los Angeles

The Daily Californian, University of California, Berkeley

Daily Texan, University of Texas, Austin

The Daily Illini, University of Illinois, Urbana-Champaign

Daily Iowan, University of Iowa, Iowa City

Daily Nebraskan, University of Nebraska, Lincoln

The Daily Pennsylvanian, University of Pennsylvania, Philadelphia

The Daily Tar Heel, University of North Carolina, Chapel Hill

Indiana Daily Student, Indiana University, Bloomington

Kansas State Collegian, Kansas State University, Manhattan

The Minnesota Daily, University of Minnesota, Twin Cities

The Red & Black, University of Georgia, Athens

The Shorthorn, University of Texas, Arlington

State Press, Arizona State University, Tempe

The University Daily Kansan, University of Kansas, Lawrence

Going into more detail on a few of these papers may help explain the qualities that make a college newspaper among the best in the country. Also, perhaps, it will suggest new ideas to papers not mentioned; so often campuses become little fiefdoms, closed off from larger social issues, not to mention the problems affecting other schools, making it hard for their papers to glean new ideas from other student newspapers.

It is this very quality of making an active effort to stay informed and keep readers informed, for example, that distinguishes the *Daily Pennsylvanian*, the only paper among our top 15 published at a private university. The *DP* staff is unusually aware of the scope of its audience. In addition to publishing the daily paper, which circulates 14,000 copies primarily on campus but also in the surrounding West Philadelphia area, the staff also produces *The Weekly Pennsylvanian*. Nearly 2,000 parents and alumni subscribe to the 8-page summary of the news from Penn's campus.

The *DP* has taken steps to ensure that the paper is relevant and reader friendly. The broadsheet is split up into standing sections, with each day highlighting a special feature. On Mondays, for example, the "Focus" page offers an in-depth look at an issue directly affecting students. In a recent issue the three stories on this page dealt with different aspects of the limits placed on minority scholarships after they were declared illegal by a Department of Education official. Tuesday's section, "The Second Degree," focuses on graduate student life and education. On Wednesdays, the "City Limits" section provides a look at issues facing the city of Philadelphia. A photo essay section, "A Thousand Words," is featured every Thursday, and Friday's "Lifestyle" section includes well-planned, original pieces on student life.

With these special sections, the *DP* staff has effectively solved the problem of serving a wide audience while maintaining a cohesive, campus-relevant product. The standing sections of the paper also address the varying needs of the audience, including the sports section's weekly "Ivy Roundup" (Ivy League standings) and daily box scores for national sports as well as thorough coverage of Penn sports.

"Off the Wire" is a daily page of stories that are, well, off the wire. A point to be made here is that while it is easy to tell when midterm week has hit many campuses by the increased number of wire stories that appear throughout the student newspaper, including on the front page, the *DP* usually confines its wire news to the allotted space even during exams.

Journalistically, the *DP* is strong. The stories are clear and concise, a reflection on both the writing and editing skills of staff members at a university where, surprisingly, there is no traditional, skills-based journalism program for undergraduates. (The Annenberg School of Communications, of which there is another at the University of Southern California, is a graduate program primarily engaged in research and policy studies.) The *DP* regularly wins top awards in national college publication contests, including the Associated Collegiate Press' National Pacemaker Award (given to the top three college newspapers in the country) for 1989-'90. This attention is particularly well-deserved since it recognizes a staff on which only editors and managers are paid, receiving nominal stipends of $90 per month.

On the other end of the economic spectrum lies the *Minnesota Daily*, where the editor in chief pulls in a higher salary than many of his counterparts at professional metropolitan papers ($21,000) and the operating budget is $2.4 million annually. (The average budget for a daily college newspaper is $800,000.) Everyone who works on the *Daily*, including free-lance writers, is paid.

Like the *DP*, the *Daily* boasts strong special sections which focus on stories that extend beyond the boundaries of campus. This includes "Worldviews," a weekly analysis of issues in countries other than the United States, written by international students. This is a concept I have seen only in the *Daily*, and it impresses me that the paper could serve to both inform and educate students with one feature, the ultimate goal for a newspaper with a large student audience.

In addition to "Worldviews," the *Daily* has a number of other editorial features that stand out. While containing comprehensive coverage of news and issues on campus, around the state and in the world, the staff also devotes a page each week to its "Words Worth" literary section. This is a forum for student poetry, stories and other art. Also, the *Daily* is one of the few college papers that have a regular book review section, featuring write-ups on books from all different genres, certainly a valuable feature to its academic market.

On the news page the *Daily* is pioneering in its coverage of gay and lesbian issues, such as domestic partnership legislation and protests against ROTC exclusionary policies. This says that the *Daily* is reaching out to expand coverage to groups that don't get a great deal of press — taking the initiative on an important civil rights issue rather than waiting for the big guys to do it first, then scurrying to catch up.

The *Daily* also is breaking ground with its photography, particularly on the sports page. Extra deadline pressure, due to night games that sometimes end minutes before the pages go out the door, has created some embarrassing holes on sports pages this year, such as the story on one school's soccer goalie accompanied by a 2-column by 6-inch box headlined "photo not available." *Daily* photographers have not fallen to the pressure, however, turning out consistently strong, active shots of all sports. Their photos, captivatingly large, focus in on the individuals involved in the play, allowing us to see the strain on the face of the football player making the tackle and the elation on the face of the diver surfacing after her meet-winning dive.

The University of Texas at Arlington's *Shorthorn* also boasts superior photography in every section. Student photojournalists there explore every possible angle in coming up with their well-composed shots, for which they regularly sweep the Rocky Mountain Collegiate Press Association photography awards. In fact, the entire paper is graphically pleasing, characterized by creative designs and clean layouts; this is a factor often overlooked in student-produced papers but as important as content in holding the reader's attention.

The *Daily Nebraskan* staff realizes the importance of incorporating good writing and good design. Their extensive use of computer graphics and illustrations breaks down information quickly and effectively, even for the student reading between classes. The headlines in the *DN* are strikingly well written, communicating the gist of the stories quickly to busy readers, and the student editors are to be commended for their aptitude in what seems to be a forgotten art. While other papers either fall back on the predictable lift-from-the-lead head or throw down dull, uninformative banners like "Students remember summer internships" or "Roommate contracts have pluses, minuses" (neither of these ran in our top 15 papers!), *DN* editors put time and thought into well-crafted, meaningful headlines. A small but telling example appeared in the January 17, 1991, issue: While the other 400 college newspapers we read slapped the word "war" in a large point size atop their lead story that day, the *DN*'s story was labeled "U.S. Storms Iraq," a clever play on the Defense Department's new code name.

War coverage invaded — and in some cases, totally engulfed — the pages of campus papers in 1991. The papers in our top 15, however, managed to preserve a balance of campus and local news in the midst of the conflict. All of them packaged the national and international news with local features, ranging from interviews with students called up for duty to those seeking conscientious objector status.

Overall our top 15 papers are noteworthy for their treatment of continuing stories, of which the gulf war is only one example. In one impressive example of investigative reporting, the *Minnesota Daily* uncovered acts of racism targeted at black students in two residence halls. Some were receiving as many as 50 death threats a week. The breaking news reports, combined with in-depth follow-up stories, brought to light a taboo subject and set the stage for a campus-wide convocation on racism. University administrators canceled classes so all students could attend the event.

The *Kansas State Collegian* provided a forum for debate when the University announced the possibility of eliminating two of K-State's eight colleges and combining several other departments. The *Collegian* became a platform for student views that otherwise might not have been heard. Following the paper's extensive coverage of both sides of the issue, the administration worked with students and elected to cancel the reorganization.

Other papers address these larger topics with special issues, such as the *The Daily Illini*'s November election issue and last fall's censorship section. These inserts are devoted entirely to meeting the particular needs of their student audiences. Several have become standing elements, such as the weekly pull-out entertainment guides in the *Daily Tar Heel* and the *Daily Nebraskan*.

These extra editions, previously the result of a semester's planning, are easier and more adaptable now since the advent of desktop publishing. Layout and design programs have changed the face of campus publications and cut production costs in the process. Now papers like the *Indiana Daily Student* can spend more of their time and revenues on color and special effects rather than pasteup and supplies.

Desktop technology has also given student newspapers a new freedom to experiment with ideas in a market where editors change yearly and procedures are not set in cement. Designs come under the scrutiny of eager eyes annually, and while the more professional among them know when to leave well enough alone, they are flexible enough to make changes when needed. In many cases, this liberty enables student publications to lead the way for professional papers — for example, many have switched completely to computerized production, while many larger professional papers remain constrained by manual paste-up.

College newspapers around the country provide valuable training grounds for tomorrow's media professionals. Student journalists are forced to juggle two full-time jobs, balancing classes with breaking news events. Editors must motivate and coddle volunteer staffs into turning out timely copy. The product they turn out has to compete daily with the electronic media, not to mention required reading assignments and term papers, to win the attention of their audience.

But when they succeed, as these 15 papers have, the results are impressive. Research shows that 92 percent of the student population read their campus newspaper each week, compared to 64 percent of the general population who read their local paper. If the success of these papers is largely a measure of their resourcefulness and their resolve — and we believe it is — the future of America's newspapers is in good hands.

Jacki Hampton is the managing editor of *U. The National College Newspaper*

11

Journalism Education:
Is There a More Meaningful "There" There?

Douglas Birkhead

The occasion for these remarks on journalism education is not exactly the war in the Persian Gulf. But as I write, planes are diving on the desert. Missiles are raining down. Troops are poised for the final penetration. Even in my remote university cubicle at the University of Utah, the war stirs an apocalyptic sensibility.

Wallace Stevens wrote of war's "immense poetry," not of the imagination, but of consciousness itself. War is the ultimate intrusive metaphor. Facts are not just facts but *heroic* facts. The media, of course, especially television, extend the intrusion beyond the battlefield and beyond the poet. All lines of awareness seem to converge. The Freedom Forum Media Studies Center's own newsletter *Communiqué* recently declared the times to be as "defining" for the mass media as for the country and world at large. As here-and-now images of war captivate us collectively in our homes, offices and schools, we are invited to trace the symmetry between epic happening and press performance, between the media's enormous capacity to dominate our attention and press responsibility.

When our political leaders speak of an emerging "New World Order," we hope they are right. Americans and others are dying for the idea, at least at this moment. But the urge to define the reporter in terms of dramatic story, as if our challenge as journalists at this unsettled time is to raise the identity of the press to the scale of heroic events, seems to confront us with an awkward solidarity. We face a kind of collaboration. When we are tempted to include the penetrating role of the media as part of the nation's ordering of the future, we weaken our commitment to examine whether our leaders are right or not. We appear to draw too close to a common center of power, perception and ideals about responsible performance. The lines of awareness we engender, even about ourselves as journalists, shouldn't converge so sharply. There shouldn't be a central focus there.

As a journalism educator, I want to write about balancing our extraordinary media efficiency and professionalism with a certain marginality, admittedly much like my own. I want to argue the virtue in preserving and teaching a detachment from the center, of isolation on the rim, perhaps even of provincialism: the "point" in having a point of view.

In contrast with Stevens' poetic fate of the observer when confronted with an epic reality, I want to introduce a more modest metaphor of engagement for journalism, and extend it to journalism education. A critic once accounted for the insight of Caribbean poet Derek Walcott by noting his existence on the periphery of empires — the British outpost of his native West Indies and the edge of American culture. This notion of seeing well from the edge, or beyond the portal but not beyond the light of the gate, is a less celebrated strategy of observation than drawing close to the center. But the perspective suggests the same source of sensibility that was the creative consolation, if not by choice, of a Ralph Ellison or James Baldwin among America's own writers. And, under the various interpretations possible for such a perspective, the outpost rather than the hub also suggests the professional station for journalists as diverse as W.E.B. DuBois, Dorothy Day and William Allen White, as well as iconoclasts such as Daniel Wolf, Max Scherr and I.F. Stone.

I am not talking about outer regions or borders strictly as sites for an alternative or regional press. A posting away from the center has a long tradition in American journalism. While the 18th-century founders of the American press were deeply and historically involved in political events, they emerged from the margins, as did the nation as a whole. Many journalists that followed continued to fashion a view from the social, cultural or political rim. Journalists of the 19th century tended to steer themselves in and out of public life; they skirted a career in letters or journeyed through other vocations. Journalism was not so much a profession as a passage along the occupational, intellectual, expressive seams of society. A worldly authority for journalism evolved not through a specific professional expertise, but because so many good journalists knew other things, and because other observers with well-traveled judgments could be journalists as well.

My purpose, of course, is to extend the metaphor one more turn. Being at the margins of two prominent and powerful social institutions — the press and the university — seems to describe the position of journalism education. The detachment is not usually taken as a fortunate expatriation, however, an opportunity for a unique monitoring role. The marginality has been the cause of perennial career anxiety. Many departments of journalism are divided into factions critically inclined to declare allegiance to one institution or the other.

This is the most familiar, and weariest, of dilemmas in journalism education. The problem essentially arises in the different orientations of educators with media credentials and those who hold communication doctorates. Neither group seems fully to appreciate the potential virtue of divided loyalties. Aggravating the situation are critics in the media and the university calling for mutually exclusive standards of teaching, service and scholarship. The difficulty reflects an ambiguity about the nature of a good journalist and a good educator. But the antagonism also stems from a common fault: the attempt to institutionalize journalism in any exclusive realm.

According to the conventional historical account, the press and higher education began their association at the turn of the century on modest but agreeable terms, exemplified by Walter Williams' newspaper laboratory at Missouri, "a real school for real newspapermen." The vocational aim of the early years was to mass-produce a standard journalist, the rules-oriented professional who could slip into any newsroom "and get away with it." The trade-school orientation perhaps reached its zenith when the University of Illinois installed punch clocks in its journalism classrooms and gave its students time cards. A cooling of the relationship is traced to criticism from wider academic circles, taunts such as Abraham Flexner's that journalism was a "make-believe" discipline; to the university career ambitions of journalism faculty; to the proliferation of graduate programs, eventually offering doctorates; to the appearance of the communication researchers of "chi-square" fame. An uneasy institutional relationship with both the press and the university, and internal factionalism, are seen as the contemporary result in journalism education.

A more formal application for admittance of the press into the academic world is represented by Joseph Pulitzer's negotiation with Columbia University to build a journalism school in New York. In addition to understanding the industrial need for trained journalists, Pulitzer also recognized the ideological coin of the emerging industrial culture. Pulitzer's endowment of the Columbia school early in the century was the symbolic equivalent in education that his World Building, the "People's Palace," had been for the skyline of the city. Both in their fashion were monuments to the institutionalization of the press, the publicity of responsible power through the prestige of architecture and higher education. Pulitzer's most significant contribution in shaping the identity of the press lay in the genius of his metaphorical investments. Endowing journalism education was just such an outlay in cultural capital.

Despite the association forged between the press and higher education, neither institution influenced the other very deeply. They were enough alike already. By the end of the 19th century, technical specialization had begun to close journalism's traditional permeability as a craft of diverse, itinerant voices, a familiar fact of industrial life. The news organization became another piece of machinery "as fine and complicated as a rotary press," in the words of muckraker Will Irwin. The press did not seek the intellectual stimulation of a university connection. Newspapers needed standardized training programs to meet new goals of industrial productivity and efficiency. Entry into the organizational press had become a management problem.

Horace White of the *New York Evening Post* touched upon the turn of affairs in commenting on Joseph Pulitzer's proposal for a journalism school. Before the rise of contemporary journalism, the press "had various aims in life, aims political, literary, scientific, social, religious reformatory and mixed, which were deemed by the conductors of the paper advantageous to the common weal," he wrote for the *North American Review* in 1904. Pulitzer's more prophetic argument in the same journal advanced a vision of the press as a "great organized force" in society. "The spirit of specialization is everywhere," he observed.

The university tradition conjures up images similar to traditional journalism's: porous institutional seams, enlightenment flowing from subject to subject, a vitality at the junctures. Such a heritage might have taken the edges off a Pulitzer. But it was not the dominant orientation of higher education at the time the press arrived at the university gate. The university had been similarly influenced by the "spirit of specialization."

Colleges were impressed by their own vigorous growth through the proliferation of disciplines. The attention of higher education was focused on new and applicable forms of professional knowledge. The institution envisioned the prospect of mass-producing a managerial class. In what historian Lawrence Vesey calls the price of structure, the modern university opted for accommodation with the organizational world, imitating its hierarchies, priority of expansion, value of efficiency through standardization and, in the name of institutional stability, its distaste for wayward license. When the press and higher education forged their inevitable union, no genesis or synthesis resulted. The cogs were made to mesh at the margins, and journalism education emerged.

Pulitzer approached the task almost as if he were letting a competitive contract. He invited the response of two universities, Columbia and Harvard. He did not approach their administrations directly but sent an emissary to visit presidents Nicholas Murray Butler of Columbia and Charles W. Eliot of Harvard. Eliot balked, not at training journalists at Harvard, but in equating journalism with the established professions. Butler hedged less. The newspaper article of their agreement that appeared in Pulitzer's *World* proclaimed the new school equal in standing to Columbia's law and other professional schools. Butler later stiffened at Pulitzer's attempt to have journalists actually control the school or to implement open admissions. The school opened after Pulitzer's death several years later, a transacted bargain between powerful equals. Eliot's legacy to journalism education was a vague ideal of individual career development, but one never worked out as a professional imperative to reorganize the management of the press.

In establishing a place in higher education, the press contracted for both social prestige and a training ground. For its part, the university acquired yet another opportunity to certify professionals and control an entry point into the career structure of society. Both institutions shared an organizational understanding of order; both promoted professional authority in society. Each penetrated the other little beyond the extent of mutual benefit.

Today, the press and the university are built on a far more comprehensive scale. They are both massive institutions, capable of being as imperious as they are bureaucratically and technologically efficient. Journalism education exists as a kind of buffer zone. But it is journalism itself that does not live in them very well. Journalism educators, instead of being factious on the periphery, should be teaching the suitability of their marginal professional life.

For most colleagues, it's easier to see the danger of identifying too closely with the press as an institution than embracing the university. The argument against the philistinism of the media industry has been made many times with great eloquence, often attached with a paean to academic life and the elevated pursuit of knowledge. Criticism of the university by media practitioners often is ignorant, offensive and anti-intellectual in tone.

But the critics are not always wrong. The university frequently treats enlightenment like a monopoly. Higher education protects its authority with acute specialization, devising arcane codes of language that turn academic departments into occult knowledge sects. Expertise often is cultivated to customize individual careers, challenging what Wendell Berry has described as the university's core mission of making humanity. Journalism educators should keep a watchful distance from both institutions.

In our long-standing plight at the margins is the potential for making a difference. In specific terms, we need to promote a more open interpretation of journalistic work than proficient and methodical news production. Good journalism often defies the rhythms of the machines inherent in the news forms we teach. We have tended to tie journalism's aims and standards of performance to organizational practices. Journalism needs a less restrictive definition and a more open community of practitioners, a sense that news relates closely to other forms of social interpretation and commentary in a broad and varied public discourse.

Journalism educators need to be more public themselves, actively engaged as academic journalists. The role ought to involve a dual competency. First, it should be a demanding craft of observation, reporting and commentary that speaks with authority in the press because its practitioners move in academic circles. Second, under the journalistic imperative for clear expression, academic journalists should be able to address university colleagues across disciplines on matters of mutual concern, opening and maintaining a sorely needed common dialogue in higher education.

In many countries around the world, journalists lead an active professional and intellectual life without a clear distinction in function. In this country, academics tend to look down on the press. Journalists often deride academic thought and expression. Nowhere else does the press have such a substantial footing in higher education, yet both our institutions tend to ignore the other's strengths for addressing precisely the deficiencies each prominently displays. Journalism education has yet to coordinate the talents of its two institutional patrons.

Where press and university meet should be a vibrant, beneficial juncture. To extend a famous line of Gertrude Stein's, journalism education need only find a more meaningful "there" there.

Douglas Birkhead is an associate professor in the department of communication at the University of Utah.

PART III

Wired Campuses

12

The World at Our Fingertips

Merrily E. Taylor

Anne Diffily, managing editor of the *Brown Alumni Monthly*, is describing her relationship with the Brown University computer network, a relationship one can only describe as addictive: "I'm a computer junkie, a network nut of the first order. Like hundreds of other users of Brown's IBM mainframe computer, I rely on such distinctly un-nerdy computer features as electronic mail and access to campus and international discussion groups to ease my work at *BAM*, to broaden my grasp of the Brown community, and to keep in touch with friends around the world." Diffily quotes Professor Litchfield of the history department for another perspective: "What I like most are the computerized library catalogs available to me at Brown, Princeton and the University of California. . . . if I am typing the footnotes for an article at 2 A.M. at home in my pajamas, and drinking cups of coffee to stay awake, and I can't remember the first name of an author, I can get the answer instantly and type it into manuscript and have everything ready to send off in the morning."

Human memory (and human nature) being what it is, most of us take the world described by Diffily and Litchfield more or less for granted. For those of us on "wired" campuses, electronic mail ("e-mail") has become a routine part of the way we do business; the personal computer with access to the network is our instrument for word processing, graphics, spreadsheet analysis and database building; and the library catalog is a resource not constrained by time or location. On some campuses, the full text of journal articles and other scholarly materials is already available via the local on-line catalog; on others, major indexes

115

and abstracting services have been mounted on the institutional mainframe as well. Universities offering this type of sophisticated information
environment range from the large (the University of Southern California)
to the small (Clemson), and from public (Georgia Institute of Technology) to private (Brown, Dartmouth College).

Libraries, always inclined by need and nature to cooperate with one
another, now find cooperation an integral part of their everyday operation, facilitated by enormous, shared bibliographic databases, global
computer networks, telefacsimile machines, and (on the horizon) the
ability to transmit documents electronically from a library workstation
to a workstation on a user's desk. For decades libraries measured status
and, to some degree, quality by the comparative size of their collections;
today this measure seems artificial, less important than an institution's
ability to retrieve information for someone regardless of where, and in
what format, that information resides. "Access," not "ownership," has
become a research library's true objective in the effort to meet scholarly
needs.

What seems hard to believe is that in the early 1980s this "world at
our fingertips" that we take so much for granted was still in many respects
the stuff that dreams — or at the very least over-optimistic visions — are
made of. Anne Diffily's routine use of the computer today, to use her own
words, represents "a revolution in scholarly research and collaboration
that has changed higher education forever."

The story of Brown's journey to today's computing and information
environment, and the library's involvement in that journey, started early
but has become typical of initiatives under way at institutions of higher
education all over the country.

Brown embarked on the "Network of Scholar's Workstations Project"
in 1983, supported by gifts from Apple, Apollo and IBM. The Apple
Education Foundation contributed 50 of its then-new Lisa computers and
worked out an agreement with the University for discount purchases of
further hardware by faculty and students; Apollo Computer donated 30
DN300 workstations. The largest gift, however, came from IBM, which
promised $15 million worth of support over three years, a significant
portion of which went to establish the University's Institute for Research
in Information and Scholarship (IRIS). IRIS would administer the computer experiment and develop software to allow a variety of workstations
to share information, to access campus mainframe databases and ser-

vices, and to communicate with distant scholars through local, state, national and international networks.

Brown had a number of strategic reasons for embarking on the project when it did. By 1983 it was not only clear that the computer was "here to stay" in higher education, but that students and faculty had increasingly complex needs: word-processing, printing and typesetting, high-speed computing, access to databases, educational and research aids, intra- and inter-campus communication, and a host of other large and small priorities. Many of these needs could no longer be met satisfactorily in the traditional mainframe environment, and it was clear that the logical move was towards "a distributed supply of services with easy access from any point on campus." By the standards of many universities at the time, faculty and students at Brown were remarkably computer literate: the late '70s and early '80s had seen what Provost Maurice Glicksman characterized as a "rapid growth in familiarity with computers"; 75 percent of the faculty at Brown, and 80 percent of the students, had already used or owned a computer.

The surge of interest in computing in higher education — and the potential market — had not been lost on the industry leaders, who in 1983 were already positioning themselves to develop a personal computer specifically targeted at faculty and students, rather than businesspeople, and who were seeking university partners in the effort. Money and equipment were available to universities willing to be on the cutting edge; the payback for the risk was the opportunity to influence the development of a proposed workstation and its software. Many university administrators saw computerization as inevitable but as something that could go awry if it were permitted to happen haphazardly, with no direction from the academy itself. Brown estimated that by 1989 it would have to spend $50 million to $70 million to make scholar's workstations available throughout the campus, but the University's suitability for the project was enhanced by its already existing campus broadband Local Area Network, BRUNET. One of the first such networks in the academic world, BRUNET in 1983 had trunk lines to 137 buildings and approximately 5,700 outlets with 1,500 working ports; although not every building was "plugged in" to the network, it was well past the experimental stage.

The fact that Brown is a liberal arts institution rather than a technical institute — and hence would be more typical of the environment to which "scholar's workstations" would eventually be marketed — was a final, crucial factor in attracting the companies involved in the project. As Apple's Steven Jobs put it at the time, "We felt that Brown, with its strong liberal arts tradition, had one of the most promising and broadly conceived approaches to the next generation of university computing." The chances were that processes, approaches and software developed at and for Brown would be applicable, and effective, in other college and university settings.

IRIS also had a sociological aspect. All parties agreed that if the workstations project developed as predicted, the changes in University life would be profound; at the same time no one was quite sure just what those changes might be. Andries van Dam, then chair of the computer science department, made a striking comparison: "It's 1905 and you have seen your first horseless carriage drive down the street. Your job is to plan the impact of this machine on the American economy, society, infrastructure. Think about what people must have felt like, the predictions they must have made. . . . I feel we don't know anything about the impact at this point."

The Brown library was a full partner in the Network of Scholar's Workstations Project from the beginning. To its credit, the University administration recognized the library as a critical academic resource whose inclusion in any list of network services would make the project attractive to many who otherwise might not have seen its usefulness to their work or research. The library, said one administrator, was "a key to the humanistic use of the workstations." When IRIS asked Brown faculty what they expected to do with their workstations, their responses — the three most frequently cited uses were word processing, e-mail and access to the library — confirmed the library's importance.

In 1983 it also seemed clear that, as the decade progressed, more and more information would become available in machine-readable form and that libraries would serve as logical "switching centers" to put users in contact with materials in a variety of formats. While a few dedicated "computer zealots" predicted (and continue to predict) the demise of print, libraries and librarians together, others recognized such a fate was unlikely — and also the value of what librarians know about how information can be organized and how people make use of it in the everyday academic setting.

A third, more political reason for having the library involved in the workstations project was the genuine concern in many minds — especially faculty — about the wisdom of the whole enterprise. Every effort had been made to make it clear that basic funding would come from outside sources, but many faculty were nonetheless alarmed by the huge expense of the project and were convinced that "computers" would eventually come to be a drain on other university priorities — not least the library. Given the library's own objectives and the community-wide belief that librarians *had* to be involved in the project if the "transformation" of Brown was to be for the better, the University librarian — me — had every reason to be an enthusiastic participant in the planning. Indeed, the library had been moving in this direction for some time.

Even before I came to Brown in 1982, the university library had decided to move away from the card catalog towards an on-line catalog. Not only was the card catalog increasingly expensive and cumbersome to maintain, but the superiority of the on-line catalog as a flexible access tool was obvious. By 1983, in fact, an on-line catalog project in itself was no longer remarkable; what was different in Brown's approach was its intention of linking that catalog with the campus network and postulating that the *primary* searching load would come through the network from remote sites, a fact which would inevitably affect screen design, user aids and so on.

Just as the Network of Scholar's Workstations Project "needed" the library, both substantively and politically, so did the library need the project, first as the mechanism by which the on-line catalog would become most useful, and second as the "hook" by which outside funding might be attracted. In 1984, then President Howard R. Swearer submitted a $1.7 million proposal to the Pew Memorial Trust, and Pew subsequently funded the on-line catalog implementation at the level of $1.5 million.

JOSIAH, the Brown University Library On-line Catalog, became available within the library in February 1988, approximately a year behind schedule, and in February 1989, after the initial "shake-down" period, the catalog was made available to the network. By summer 1990 the database had reached some 860,000 records — it now approaches a million — and in the period between September 1989 and May 1990, JOSIAH entertained some 568,716 searches. In late '89 JOSIAH became available on Internet, the National Science Foundation-sponsored network, and now averages around 4,500 searches a day from both the campus network and elsewhere. The on-line catalog has become the University's largest and most visible academic system, and an indispensable part of campus life. Last winter the library and the University's division of Computing and Information Services (CIS) began negotiations with a major international software vendor to share in the development of a new integrated library system, working in concert with three other major universities. The new system will include a full-text retrieval module to enable the loading of large information databases, such as MEDLINE, and is slated for testing in 1991-92.

But we didn't stop with the on-line catalog: Last fall the library and CIS completed installation of a CD-Rom network, which, when fully operational, will enable approximately 600 personal computers campuswide to search databases on 21 disks mounted on a library file server.

In addition to its more tangible gains through the Network of Scholar's Workstations Project, the Brown library has achieved clear recognition as a major player, now and in the future, in the University's planning for the acquisition and management of scholarly information in electronic form. In the fall of 1988, the University's policy on "access to electronic information" established as a principle that "information, regardless of format, should be viewed as a University-wide resource available to all members of the community," and further that "by both custom and policy, the University library serves as the official custodian for the institution's store of recorded information. . . . only the University library is charged formally with acquiring material, organizing it, maintaining it, and taking steps to see that it is readily available to all members of our academic community. The mode of storage of information (i.e. electronic vs. traditional format) does not alter the need for these basic functions, which historically have well served the University community."

It is worth noting at this point that the historic commitment of libraries and librarians to the mission of collecting and preserving information — and most importantly, making it available for use — must not be undervalued or overlooked as universities move forward into a new era of scholarly communication. While other agencies and individuals on campus acquire, utilize and value scholarly information, only the library has those roles as its single, overriding purpose. Furthermore, librarians may be the only professionals on campus with a "global view" as to how students, faculty, researchers and scholars in all fields seek and use information in a *variety of formats*. For these and other reasons, librarians cannot be bit players in the drama of transforming the campus through access to networked information; they should — indeed, must — play a leading role.

What about the Network of Scholar's Workstations Project itself? Was it a success? In terms of the end result, the answer has to be "yes" — although as is frequently the case in great endeavors, our success wasn't quite what we expected. Brian Hawkins, Brown's vice president for Computing and Information Services, says that when the University began the project the emphasis was on a "Network of *Scholar's Work-stations*," when in fact the real transformation of the University was brought about by the "*Network* of Scholar's Workstations." The work-station that Brown envisioned in the early days of the project never materialized; instead, the Macintosh and the IBM-PC proved to be the workstations that captured the market and that faculty, students and staff embraced. Neither did workstations proliferate on campus as quickly as we first predicted, not least because the original architects of the project had considerably underestimated the difficulty not only of developing the workstation but of dealing with the myriad details involved in establishing them in academic departments — installing connections to the network, acquiring peripheral items like printers, computer tables and modems, training faculty, students and support staff, and so on.

Neither did the "sociological" side of IRIS develop as expected; despite the University's conviction that it was important to identify and document the changes in academic life brought about by computeriza-tion, it proved impossible to clearly articulate the focus of such research, and consequently it was difficult to raise money to support it. Nonetheless a number of useful studies *were* done, including a baseline survey of the University community and its computer use that provided the foundation for a series of continuing surveys, and a study of the library in transition. But the larger picture of the University's transformation was never recorded in the full-scale, systematic manner that future scholars — or administrators — might have found useful.

Undeniably, however, academic life at Brown *has* been transformed, and in many of the ways predicted by the "prophets" of the early 1980s. Today the University supports seven miles of backbone cable and 150 miles of auxiliary cable linking more than 100 buildings on campus. Approximately 7,000 workstations and other devices can access the network, 3,000 of them University-owned, 4,000 owned by faculty and students. One administrator at Brown has speculated that the University is one of the nation's leaders in making workstations available to students; 97 percent of them use a computer in some fashion, and the average student spends about 8.5 hours a week working on a computer. As of September 1990, 1,000 people — students, staff and faculty — were making use of BRUNO, the University's conferencing and news system, which provides everything from a bulletin board service to private conferences for students, administrators, faculty and other working groups.

As for faculty, a survey undertaken in November 1990 revealed that 97 percent of all full-time faculty use a computer weekly or more often; 88 percent indicated that computers were critical to their research, and 75 percent said they had purchased a computer for home use. Interestingly, while a high percentage of faculty professed interest in and support for the computer as a teaching tool, the percentage of the faculty who reported actually *using* it that way was much lower: 25 percent of the faculty made assignments requiring use of the computer, and only 20 percent used the computer in the classroom. Those analyzing the survey concluded, perhaps unsurprisingly, that "younger academics are more inclined to think of this technology as a teaching tool than their older colleagues."

Just how do faculty make use of the network for their own scholarship and research? Bill Ellis, associate professor of English and American studies at Pennsylvania State University, uses computer conferences and e-mail to track down material on his field of interest, legends. Many faculty members fire off questions on specific scholarly problems to their e-mail colleagues; others use the network as a mechanism for joint work on papers or other projects (including high-speed "number-crunching" on a distant supercomputer). Some publishers now accept manuscripts submitted on-line. Brown's Women Writers Project, which is locating and putting into electronic form texts by early women writers in English, hopes one day "to place all of the electronic texts the WWP is creating onto an Internet file server, where they will be fully available and searchable by scholars and institutions around the world." Through the Coalition for Networked Information — a joint project of the Association of Research Libraries, EDUCOM and CAUSE — the Brown University library and CIS division are working to make sure that information available on Internet is made accessible to scholars in the most straightforward and "user-friendly" manner possible. Faculty might one day, for example, find pointers to texts from the Women Writers Project in their own local on-line catalogs, regardless of where the Internet file server is actually located.

If the Network of Scholar's Workstations project succeeded, in the course of eight years, in changing the nature of academic and social life at Brown, one can only speculate about the future impact of the world-wide computer network that already exists and that promises to become ever more significant in the next decade. BITNET, the higher education network created in 1981 by Ira H. Fuchs, then vice chancellor of the City University of New York, already links some 3,000 sites around the world for e-mail and file transfer only. Of even greater significance is Internet, "a global network that links a number of regional networks . . . estimated to link well over 100,000 computers around the world." It is through Internet that Brown faculty and students may access other library on-line catalogs, take advantage of supercomputers, send large files back and forth, and in other ways inhabit a scholarly world free of the constraints of time and space. Senator Albert Gore of Tennessee has recently introduced a bill that would essentially convert Internet into NREN — the National Research and Education Network. When and if NREN comes to be, it would be bigger than any network to date, "a national highway system for data." Brown students and faculty who now enjoy use of the campus network may, within a few short years, take for granted the availability of a network connection in their own homes. When that day comes, the changes in daily life in the United States will be as profound as those that have come to Brown in the decade of the '80s.

Merrily E. Taylor is the Brown University librarian.

13

The Silicon Scholar

William H. Graves

The computer's educational potential, for years more promise than reality, began to blossom in the 1980s. The personal computer, interactive technology's most affordable incarnation, made it possible to reorganize and manipulate the results of computation and information retrieval for presentation at the desktop, a capacity that enlivens reading, listening, viewing and computing — learning — in today's engaging multimedia environments.

In the 1990s, the educational potential of information technology will be heightened by the democratizing capability of networks to summon information instantaneously from afar. Digital telecommunication and networking technologies are combining with the most exciting forms of personal computing to open new communications possibilities, and the academic ascendance of interpersonal computing is well under way, guided by work initiated at a few universities in the '80s. Members of the academic community are now seeking new tools for connecting to a growing global body of information resources and for communicating with each other — scholar to scholar, teacher to student, and student to student. Encouraged by the Apple Macintosh, the IBM/Microsoft Windows system and a range of graphical UNIX workstations, they expect seamless interconnectivity to people and resources, and they expect all of this, consciously or unconsciously, in an open, heterogeneous environment. The focus is on information, whether in traditional or new multimedia formats, and on the tools to interpret it, transform it and share it with others — all at the click of a mouse button, the touch of finger on screen, the stroke of pen on digital tablet, or the digital recognition of audible command from human to machine.

Today's exemplary trends suggest tomorrow's more pervasive possibilities — and the barriers to their fulfillment. Harnessing the imminent convergence of multimedia-enhanced personal computing and wide-area digital networking will require new collaborative models of competition in the information technology and education "industries" and massive investments in physical infrastructure in the nation's schools, colleges and universities.

One of the most powerful themes of current educational experimentation with interactive technologies is the introduction of the active practice of a discipline or profession into the classroom. It is increasingly unnecessary, in a variety of disciplinary and professional contexts, to lecture about problem-solving techniques and practices while patronizing students with restricted or grossly diminished problem-solving opportunities. Instead, students with access to the same problem-solving tools used by their mentors can be expected to tackle "real" problems. At the same time, technology is changing the nature of creativity and hence of the problems tackled by academics. If computer algebra systems make obsolete traditional problem sets in calculus, what is the calculus course? If technology can produce an entire musical score from a single chord, who (or what) is the creator, and what is a "composition"?

While the debate about the tension between teaching and research rages, some technologically proficient scholars are quietly utilizing technology to introduce active scholarship into the undergraduate curriculum. This development has the curious effect of confirming the research universities' claim that "research informs teaching" while also suggesting how any college or university can use networks to share in this advantage.

One such project is CUPLE (Comprehensive Unified Physics Learning Environment), developed by a consortium led by Professors Chad McDaniel and Joe Redish of the University of Maryland and Professor Jack Wilson of Rensselaer Polytechnic Institute, and supported by the American Association of Physics Teachers, the Annenberg/CPB Project and IBM. CUPLE integrates interactive texts, computational modeling, data collection and analysis, video from disks and tapes as sources of information and data, and a variety of software tools into an IBM PS/2 environment in which undergraduates learn physics by doing physics.

Similarly, at the University of Illinois Professors Horacio Porta and Jerry Uhl prefer coaching calculus to lecturing about it. Their calculus class is conducted as a laboratory in which students seated at Macintoshes engage in dynamic experimentation and problem-solving. With support from Addison-Wesley, Apple and Wolfram Research, Porta and Uhl (and their student Donald Brown) are experimenting with the educational potential of Wolfram's powerful computer algebra system, *Mathematica*, to produce a new interactive calculus text, which they describe in visionary terms:

> Imagine a mathematics text in which each example is infinitely many examples because each example can be redone immediately by the student with new numbers and functions. Imagine a symbolic or numerical computer routine into which fully word-processed descriptions can be inserted at will between lines of active code. Imagine a text whose paragraphs can be modified and added to as the teacher sees fit. Imagine a text that has better graphics and plots than any available in any standard mathematics book, and imagine that the amount of graphics is limited only by the computer memory instead of the cost and weight of printed pages. Imagine that all graphics can be in color and that three-dimensional graphics are all perfectly shaded and can easily be viewed from any desired viewpoint. Imagine a text in which the student can find as much space as he or she needs to solve the assigned exercises. Imagine that a student, in a matter of seconds, can copy his or her own homework and can turn it in while retaining the original.

Teachers transformed from lecturers to coaches, students transformed from passive recipients to active participants, and serial text enlivened by interactivity and the possibilities of the graphical multimedia screen: these are the immediate educational horizons.

Nor are the prospects limited to the sciences. Technology has enhanced foreign language teaching since the introduction of the language lab, and now that venerable institution is responding to the query-driven educational opportunities inherent in electronic databases. Word processors enriched by spelling checkers, thesauruses, and limited keyboard support for foreign languages are commonplace, but Cornell Professors James Noblitt and Donald Sola and Dr. Willem Pet, supported by IBM, have developed a writing tool more useful to language students: *Systeme D*, an award-winning bilingual word processor that features a bilingual dictionary and a context-sensitive database of verb forms, vocabulary items, phrases and examples of usage. Noblitt and Pet are working with Professor Bernard Petit of SUNY-Brockport to combine the editing and querying features of *Systeme D* with "windowed" videodisc clips organized interactively by listening-comprehension problems and cultural contexts.

The Perseus Project, supported by the Annenberg/CPB Project and Apple, is a similar information resource in the classics. Under the editorship of Harvard Professor Gregory Crane, *Perseus* was developed using the information-management program *Hypercard* to give the "reader" nonlinear "hyper" access to a database of texts, dictionaries, images (maps, site and building plans, art), and videodisc sequences on the classical Greek world. *Perseus* is an electronic journal and small library awaiting queries from student and scholar alike.

The databases in *Systeme D* and *Perseus* are information resources that should be available to scholars and students on a national network. There are as well many other databases too extensive to be stored on a microcomputer — census data, for example — and which will be available only to a select few researchers and students until personal computing and wide-area networking converge in a national network accessible from most academic desktops.

That day may come soon. Currently Internet is the nation's academic network, an aggregate of local and regional networks that incorporates the National Science Foundation's national backbone, NSFnet, and connects researchers and resources across the country (and the world). But if Senator Albert Gore's bill prevails in Congress, Internet will become NREN (the National Research and Education Network), which will be the leading developmental edge of a national, probably privatized, communications infrastructure. Three academic organizations — EDUCOM, CAUSE (both groups that support information technology in higher education) and the Association of Research Libraries (ARL) — have formed the Coalition for Networked Information (CNI) to help develop the "Education" in NREN and to ensure attention to information access and content, as well as to high-performance computation.

Work under way by Professor Frank Dominguez of the University of North Carolina at Chapel Hill and Dr. Peter Batke of Johns Hopkins University, both fellows at UNC's Institute for Academic Technology, highlights CNI's concerns. Together they created an electronic critical edition of a 15th-century Spanish poem written by Jorge Manrique. Working on an IBM PS/2, they used the hypertext features of *ToolBook* to achieve a new kind of cross-referencing and linking of textual materials in a digital edition that is richer and more flexible than a printed one.

Accompanying a scanned image of Manrique's original text (complete with woodcuts) are several interpretations and translations entered through *ToolBook*'s editing facilities. "Hyperannotation" makes notes available to the reader on demand but does not demand that the reader view them, and the reader can zoom in on particular features of the original text and woodcuts with the click of a mouse. In such an electronic critical edition, one scholar can add to the work of others to create a dynamic, living "text."

Here again, scholars are fulfilling their roles as teachers by using interactive technology to incorporate authentic scholarship into the student experience. The Manrique example, after all, is not an electronic lesson or tutorial. It is an annotated collection of primary and secondary source materials as readily available to students as to the scholars who created it. Such electronic critical editions should become widely available and increasingly malleable if NREN becomes a reality.

But this prospect raises questions that stir commercial publishers, librarians and scholars. Who will own these new texts? Who will distribute them? Who will have access to them on the network and at what, if any, cost? Who will have the right to amend or edit them? How will they be incorporated in an academic vita? How will they be considered by tenure and promotion committees? What will be the nature of the collections at major research libraries? Who will have access to them and from where?

Commercial publishers, for the most part, are taking a conservative approach to electronic publication. Some have taken the first step of distributing curriculum materials on diskette (educational software), but these electronic materials often are distributed with printed materials to stimulate and protect significant sales — for example, about $1.3 million annually alone in the market for freshman biology texts. With that in mind, Addison-Wesley publishes its interactive calculus text accompanied by the "real McCoy" on diskette. A few companies are forming electronic publication divisions (Heinle and Heinle, for example, publishes *Systeme D*), and one forward-looking company, Course Technologies, was created solely to publish curricular software for higher education, its bread-and-butter business the creation and distribution of printed curriculum materials to accompany popular productivity software, such as *Lotus 1-2-3*. Some disciplinary societies, such as the Modern Language Association, are experimenting with on-line publication of journal materials — full texts in a few cases but mostly indexes and abstracts. In the wings is the world's leading software company, Microsoft, with its *Bookshelf* of reference materials available on CD-ROM and, no doubt, its eye on the networked distribution of electronic reference materials of broad appeal.

Academic books currently come in two economic flavors: textbooks for the free-market economy of introductory courses, and specialized books that depend for their existence on the library market or the only slightly broader market that sustains university presses. Most commercial activity with electronic materials appears to target the free market, and thus it is reasonable to reflect on the electronic equivalent of the development of a freshman textbook.

Traditionally such a textbook evolves from class notes that grow and are polished over several terms of teaching the same course. The electronic counterpart might then be the interactive text that evolves from "hypernotes" in the same way. The Addison-Wesley interactive calculus text is an example. Most teachers are more likely to make the incremental move to "hyperlecturing" than the leap to full-blown software development, and tools such as *Hypercard* and *ToolBook* are sufficiently powerful and easy to use that lecturers can safely prepare hyperlectures at 10:30 p.m. before the next day's classes.

Until most educational software can be used in "10:30 P.M. mode," only a few heat-seeking teachers will use technology-based materials in their courses, and even then their institutions will have to invest in appropriate classroom, lab and networking technologies to make them effective. Such infrastructure issues have implications beyond the individual campus and will require opening the borders that have traditionally separated the academic and the corporate communities.

The reign of centralized computing was overthrown on many college and university campuses in the 1980s, turned out by the democratizing effects of the personal computing revolution and its aftermath, *laissez-faire*-distributed computing. This in turn is now being reined into the "federal model," in which central information technology organizations are responsible for campus-wide data and communications systems that will ensure institutional coherence while enabling and encouraging individual and departmental initiatives. The next step is a pan-campus infrastructure — a "national federal model" — that will enable national sharing of information resources and services and that will provide economic incentives for the costly development of resources and services for the common educational good. This is one of the keystones of NREN and its propelling partnership between multicampus organizations (ARL, CAUSE, EDUCOM), the government, and the information technology industry.

But a pan-campus infrastructure demands some modification to traditional free-market competitive practices in the information technology industry. NREN will address only its "Research" — sophisticated, high-performance computational needs — unless vendors cooperate in several critical areas. For example, the development of interactive multimedia materials is costly and thus very risky in an environment in which there are no standards to ensure that materials developed on one multimedia configuration will run on others. Industry-based organizations such as the Interactive Multimedia Association (IMA), which has attracted such competing heavyweights as Apple, IBM and Microsoft to the quest for interoperability, offer a possible solution. Competitors naturally find such cooperative ventures difficult to craft and sustain, but the payoff could be a business opportunity open to all cooperating companies — in the case of IMA, a sizable market for multimedia applications. Such standards for interoperability are key to the "Education" in NREN, and so are part of its infrastructure. Educators can hope that IMA and similar efforts will hasten the broader collaborations between industry, education and government required for a national information infrastructure.

But just as competitors in the information technology industry are beginning to collaborate for the common good, government is stridently advocating a free-market approach to education. Only the fittest schools will survive under President Bush's policy of "choice," a policy aimed chiefly at primary and secondary public schools but which has its advocates for the higher education "market" as well. Such an approach utterly ignores the complexity of infrastructure issues.

In a recent *Wall Street Journal* article on "techno-choice," "Luddite Schools Wage a Wasteful War," Lewis J. Perelman argued that "U.S. public schools and colleges are technologically stuck in the Middle Ages for the same reason Soviet collective farms are: a complete lack of accountability to the consumer and total insulation from competitive market forces." If U.S. colleges are technologically caught in the Middle Ages — though earlier examples in these pages might suggest pockets of 20th-century activity and 21st-century direction — then "total insulation from competitive market forces" is not a cause.

Colleges and universities, whether private or state-supported, compete vigorously for the best students (and scholars). Perelman's point that current educational practice largely ignores the proven potential of a variety of interactive technologies to increase educational productivity and quality is well taken — though he comes perilously close to equating training with education. But there is more to the issue than "Luddite schools." Infrastructure — or rather the lack of it — is a critical impediment to the broad diffusion of educational innovation.

To take but one example: During the past decade, the University of North Carolina has experimented successfully with "computing across the curriculum," but success has depended on funding from the corporate community and on small, one-time state allocations. To sustain and extend the educational gains will require creating an information technology infrastructure conservatively estimated to include $25 million in capital costs and $2.5 million in new operating expenses for the campus. Campuses are facing such demands nationwide, but they come at a time when government and governing bodies at all levels — from school boards to boards of governors, from the Department of Education to the White House — exhibit little understanding of the scope and complexity of today's technological opportunity to improve education. (UNC's budget for information technology, for example, remained flat for several years before being reduced last year when North Carolina's political leadership opted for budget cuts over increased taxes to meet revenue shortfalls.) Even the most technologically enlightened educational leaders will find it impossible in the foreseeable future to reallocate existing funds in the amounts required to meet new technology-based educational opportunities. What, then, can be done?

Most important, perhaps, Perelman's "consumers" are voters who must come to believe in the role of information technology as a vital catalyst for educational quality worthy of federal, state and local investment. His "techno-choice" education will otherwise be feasible only in the most affluent school districts, colleges and universities. (In Perelman's free-market road to educational quality, it will "take money to make money.")

Collaboration between the academic community and the private sector — such as the Coalition on Educational Initiatives sponsored by Coca-

Cola, IBM and Proctor & Gamble for the benefit of the public schools, or higher education's EDUCOM Award Program supported by a host of "high-tech" companies — is also a key to redeeming the educational promise of technology. All of the examples described in this article involve academic/corporate collaboration. The IBM-supported Institute for Academic Technology is operated by the University of North Carolina on the basis of mutual benefit: Technology marketed to higher education is most likely to meet academic needs if a national cross section of academics has a voice in its design and function, and information exchange about the academic uses of technology is most likely to respond to educational priorities if designed and delivered by academics.

The scope of such collaboration spans the spectrum of educational goals and institutions. The Massachusetts Institute of Technology's Project Athena, supported by Digital and IBM, has pointed the way toward a "networked" campus of powerful workstations supporting all aspects of teaching, learning and research. IBM-sponsored Project Synergy, based at Miami-Dade Community College and involving other community colleges, is bringing technology to bear on the development of students' basic academic skills.

The educational potential of interactive technologies has never been stronger. Much has been accomplished, but an infrastructure investment of national scope is a prerequisite for further progress on a national scale. This will require new forms of collaboration across the corporate, public and academic sectors. The moment demands no less.

William H. Graves is associate provost for information technology and professor of mathematics at the University of North Carolina at Chapel Hill, where he is also chairman of the national advisory board for the University's Institute for Academic Technology.

PART IV

Free Expression on Campus

14

How Free Is Higher Education?

Howard Zinn

In early 1950, Congressman Harold Velde of Illinois, rising in the House of Representatives to oppose mobile library service to rural areas, told his colleagues: "The basis of communism and socialistic influence is education of the people."

That warning was uttered in the special climate of the Cold War, but education has always inspired fear among those who want to keep the existing distributions of power and wealth as they are.

In my 30 years of teaching — in a small southern college, in a large northeastern university — I have often observed that fear. And I think I understand what it is based on. The educational environment is unique in our society: it is the only situation where an adult, looked up to as a mentor, is alone with a group of young people for a protracted and officially sanctioned period of time and can assign whatever reading he or she chooses, and discuss with these young people any subject under the sun. The subject may be defined by the curriculum, by the catalog course description, but this is a minor impediment to a bold and imaginative teacher, especially in literature, philosophy and the social sciences, where there are unlimited possibilities for free discussion of social and political issues.

That would seem to be an educational ideal — an arena for free discussion, assuming a diversity of viewpoints from a variety of teachers, of the most important issues of our time. Yet it is precisely that situation, in the classrooms of higher education, which frightens the guardians of the status quo.

They declare their admiration for such freedom in principle, and suggest that radicals are insufficiently grateful for its existence. But when teachers actually *use* this freedom, introducing new subjects, new readings, outrageous ideas, challenging authority, criticizing "Western civilization," amending the "canon" of great books as listed by certain educational authorities of the past — then the self-appointed guardians of "high culture" become enraged.

Early in my teaching career I decided that I would make the most of the special freedom that is possible in a classroom. I would introduce what I felt to be the most important, and therefore the most controversial, questions in my classes.

When I was assigned, as a young professor at Spelman College, a college for black women in Atlanta, a course in "Constitutional Law," I changed the course title to "Civil Liberties" and departed from the canonized recital of Supreme Court cases. I did not ignore the most important of these cases, but I also talked with the students about social movements for justice and asked what role these movements played in changing the environment within which Supreme Court decisions were made.

When I taught American history, I ignored the canon of the traditional textbook, in which the heroic figures were mostly presidents, generals and industrialists. In those texts, wars were treated as problems in military strategy and not in morality; Christopher Columbus and Andrew Jackson and Theodore Roosevelt were treated as heroes in the march of democracy, with not a word from the objects of their violence.

I suggested that we approach Columbus and Jackson from the perspective of their victims, that we look at the magnificent feat of the transcontinental railroad from the viewpoint of the Irish and Chinese laborers who, in building it, died by the thousands.

Was I committing that terrible sin which is arousing the anger of today's fundamentalists — "politicizing the curriculum"? Is there any rendition of constitutional law, any recounting of American history that can escape being *political* — that is, expressing a political point of view? To treat Theodore Roosevelt as a hero (which is usually not done overtly, but in an expression of quiet admiration) — is that less "political" than pointing to his role as an early imperialist, a forerunner of a long string of crude U.S. interventions in the Caribbean?

I have no doubt that I was taking a political stand when, in the early 1960s, I expressed respect for my students who missed classes to demonstrate in downtown Atlanta against racial segregation. In doing that, was I being more political than the fundamentalist Allen Bloom, at Cornell, who pointed with pride to the fact that the students in his seminar on Plato and Aristotle stuck to their studies and refused to participate in the social conflict outside the seminar room?

In my teaching I never concealed my political views: my detestation of war and militarism, my anger at racial inequality, my belief in a democratic socialism, in a rational and just distribution of the world's wealth. To pretend to an "objectivity" that was neither possible nor desirable seemed to me dishonest.

I made it clear to my students at the start of each course that they would be getting *my* point of view on the subjects under discussion, that I would try to be fair to other points of view, that I would scrupulously uphold their right to disagree with me. (I understand that radicals too can become dogmatic and intolerant, or — and I'm not sure which is worse — recondite in their pretentious theorizing — but these are traits one finds at all points on the political spectrum.)

My students had a long experience of political indoctrination before they arrived in my class — in the family, in high school, in movies and television. They would hear viewpoints other than mine in other courses, and for the rest of their lives. I insisted on my right to enter my opinions in the marketplace of ideas, so long dominated by orthodoxy.

Surely the expression of "political views" (what is just, or unjust? what can citizens do?) is inevitable in education. It may be done overtly, honestly, or it may be there subtly. But it is always there, however the textbook, by its very bulk and dullness, pretends to neutrality, however noncommittal is the teacher.

It is inevitably there because all education involves *selection* — of events, of voices, of books — and any insistence on one list of great books or great figures or great events is a partial (in both senses of that term) rendering of our cultural heritage.

Therefore it seems to me that the existence of free expression in higher education must mean the opportunity for many points of view, many political biases, to be presented to students. This requires a true pluralism of readings, ideas, viewpoints — a genuinely free marketplace of thought and culture. Let both Shakespeare and Wole Soyinka, Bach and Leonard

Bernstein, Dickens and W.E.B. Du Bois, John Stuart Mill and Zora Neale Hurston, Rembrandt and Picasso, Plato and Lao-tzu, Locke and Marx, Aeschylus and August Wilson, Jane Austen and Gabriel García Marquez be available to students.

Such a free marketplace of ideas does not depend essentially on "the curriculum." How many words have been wasted moving those empty shells around the debating table! What is crucial is the content of those shells, which depends on who the teachers are and who the students are. A thoughtful teacher can take a course labeled "Western Civilization" and enlarge its content with an exciting global perspective. Another teacher can be given a course grandly called "World Civilization" and give the student an eclectic, limp recounting of dull events and meaningless dates.

That pluralism in thought that is required for truly free expression in higher education has never been realized. Its crucial elements — an ideologically diverse faculty, a heterogeneous student body (in class, race, sex — those words that bring moans from the keepers of the "higher culture") have always been under attack from outside and from inside the colleges and universities.

McCarthyism — in which the corporate nature of academic institutions revealed itself in the surrender of university administrators to government inquisitors (see Ellen Schrecker's book *No Ivory Tower: McCarthyism in the Universities* for the details) — was only the most flagrant of the attacks on freedom of expression. More subtle, more persistent, has been the control of faculty appointments, contract renewals and tenure (inevitably with political considerations) by colleagues, but especially by administrators, who are the universities' links with the dominant forces of American society — the government, the corporations, the military.

Boston University, where I taught for many years, is not too far from typical, with its panoply of military and government connections — ROTC chapters for every military service, former government officials given special faculty posts, the board of trustees dominated by corporate executives, a president eager to curry favor with powerful politicos. Almost all colleges and universities are organized as administrative hierarchies in which a president and trustees, usually well connected to wealthy and important people in the outside world, make the critical decisions as to who may enjoy the freedom of the classroom to speak to the young people of the new generation.

Higher education, while enjoying some special privileges, is still part of the American system, which is an ingenious, sophisticated system of control. It is not totalitarian; what permits it to be called a democracy is that it allows apertures of liberty on the supposition that this will not endanger the basic contours of wealth and power in the society. It trusts that the very flexibility of a partially free system will assure its survival, even contribute to its strength.

Our government is so confident of its power that it can risk allowing some political choice to the people, who can vote for Democrats or Republicans but find huge obstacles of money and bureaucracy if they want an alternative. Our corporations are so wealthy that they can afford some distribution of wealth to a supportive middle class, but not to the 30 or 40 million people who live in the cellars of society.

The system can allow special space for free expression in its cultural institutions — the theater, the arts, the media. But the size of that space is controlled by money and power; the profit motive limits what is put on stage or screen; government officials dominate the informational role of the news media.

Yes, there is, indeed, a special freedom of expression in the academy. How can I at Boston University, or Noam Chomsky at MIT, or David Montgomery at Yale, deny that we have had more freedom in the university than we would have in business or other professions? But those who tolerate us know that our numbers are few, that our students, however excited by new ideas, go out into a world of economic pressures and exhortations to caution. And they know too that they can point to us as an example of the academy's openness to all ideas.

True, there is a tradition of academic freedom, but it is based on a peculiar unspoken contract. The student, in return for the economic security of a career and several years with some degree of free intellectual play, is expected upon graduation to become an obedient citizen, partic-ipating happily in the nation's limited pluralism (be a Republican or a Democrat, but please, nothing else).

The boundaries for free expression in the university, though broader than in the larger society, are still watched carefully. When that freedom is used, even by a small minority, to support social change considered dangerous by the guardians of the status quo, the alarm goes out: "The

Communists are infiltrating our institutions"; "Marxists have taken over the curriculum"; "feminists and black militants are destroying classical education."

Their reaction approaches hysteria: "With a few notable exceptions, our most prestigious liberal arts colleges and universities have installed the entire radical menu at the center of their humanities curriculum," says Roger Kimball in his book *Tenured Radicals*. The shrillness of such alarms is never proportionate to the size of the radical threat. But the Establishment takes no chances. Thus J. Edgar Hoover and Joseph McCarthy saw imminent danger of communist control of the U.S. government; protectors of "the canon" see "tenured radicals" taking over higher education. The axes then get sharpened.

Yes, some of us radicals have somehow managed to get tenure. But far from dominating higher education, we remain a carefully watched minority. Some of us may continue to speak and write and teach as we like, but we have seen the axe fall countless times on colleagues less lucky. And who can deny the chilling effect this has had on other faculty, with or without tenure, who have censored themselves rather than risk a loss of promotion, a lower salary, a nonrenewal of contract, a denial of tenure?

Perhaps, after all, Boston University cannot be considered typical, having had for 20 years probably the most authoritarian, the most politically watchful university president in the country. But although it is hard to match John Silber as an educational tyrant, he can be considered (I base this on spending some time at other universities) not a departure from the norm, but an exaggeration of it.

Have we had freedom of expression at Boston University?

A handful of radical teachers, in a faculty of over a thousand, was enough to have John Silber go into fits over our presence on campus, just as certain observers of higher education are now getting apoplectic over what they see as radical dominance nationwide. These are ludicrous fantasies, but they lead to attacks on the freedom of expression of those faculty who manage to overcome that prudent self-control so prominent among academics. At Boston it must have been such fantasies that led Silber to determinedly destroy the faculty union, which was a minor threat to his control over faculty. He handled appointments and tenure with the very political criteria that his conservative educational companions so loudly decry. In at least seven cases that I know of, where the candidates were politically undesirable by Silber's standards, he ignored overwhelming faculty recommendations and refused them tenure.

Did I have freedom of expression in my classroom? I did, because I followed Aldous Huxley's advice: "Liberties are not given; they are taken." But it was obviously infuriating to John Silber that every semester 400 students signed up to take my courses, whether it was "Law and Justice in America" or "An Introduction to Political Theory." And so he did what is often done in the academy; he engaged in petty harassments —withholding salary raises, denying teaching assistants. He also threatened to fire me (and four other members of the union) when we held our classes on the street rather than cross the picket lines of striking secretaries.

The fundamentalists of politics — the Reagans and Bushes and Helmses — want to pull the strings of control tighter on the distribution of wealth and power and civil liberties. The fundamentalists of law, the Borks and Rehnquists, want to interpret the Constitution so as to put strict limits on the legal possibilities for social reform. The fundamentalists of education fear the possibilities inherent in the unique freedom of discussion that we find in higher education.

And so, under the guise of defending "the common culture" or "disinterested scholarship" or "Western civilization," they attack that freedom. They fear exactly what some of us hope for, that if students are given wider political choices in the classroom than they get in the polling booth or the workplace, they may become social rebels. They may join movements for racial or sexual equality, or against war, or, even more dangerous, work for what James Madison feared as he argued for a conservative Constitution, "an equal division of property."

We have some freedom, but it needs to be guarded and expanded. As Bertolt Brecht wanted to say but was prevented from saying to his inquisitors of the House Committee on Un-American Activities: "We are living in a dangerous world. Our state of civilization is such that mankind already is capable of becoming enormously wealthy but as a whole is still poverty-ridden. Great wars have been suffered. Greater wars are imminent, we are told. Do you not think that in such a predicament every new idea should be examined carefully and freely?"

Howard Zinn is professor emeritus of political science at Boston University.

15

The Tyranny of Virtue

Roger Kimball

Is higher education the leading institutional champion of free expression in American society? Consider a few recent episodes on American campuses:

- At the University of Pennsylvania, a student on a panel for "diversity education" wrote a memorandum to her colleagues in which she expressed her "deep regard for the individual and . . . desire to protect the freedoms of all members of society." A university administrator responded by circling the passage just quoted, underlining the word 'individual,' and commenting, "This is a 'RED FLAG' phrase today, which is considered by many to be RACIST. Arguments that champion the individual over the group ultimately privileges [sic] the 'individuals' belonging to the largest or dominant group."

- The University of Michigan had enacted an "anti-harassment" policy that prohibited speech that "stigmatizes or victimizes an individual on the basis of race, ethnicity, religion, sex, sexual orientation, creed, national origin, ancestry, age, marital status, handicap, or Vietnam-era veteran status." Examples of proscribed speech included "Your student organization sponsors a comedian who slurs Hispanics" and "A male student makes remarks in class like 'women just aren't as good in this field as men.'" This policy was so vague and all-encompassing that it was eventually thrown out by a federal judge.

- Tufts University recently decreed that the speech of its students and faculty will be regulated according to zone. In public areas, speech is unregulated; in classrooms, libraries and dining halls, "derogatory and demeaning speech" is subject to punitive action; and in dormitories, offensive remarks held to violate a student's "right to privacy" are liable to punishment.

Students have wryly dubbed these zones the "Free Speech Zone," the "Limited Speech Zone" and the "Twilight Zone."

• The University of Connecticut has outlawed "harassment," defined as "all remarks that offend or stigmatize women or minorities," including "the use of derogatory names," "inconsiderate jokes," and even "conspicuous exclusion from conversation." Penalties range from reprimand to expulsion.

Far from being atypical, these examples epitomize current efforts to enforce "politically correct" thinking on campuses across the country. Undertaken in the name of multiculturalism, diversity, pluralism and other virtuous-sounding abstractions, the campaign for PC-hood underscores the extent to which higher education in this country has been transformed into a species of ideological indoctrination — a continuation of politics by other means.

As Alan Charles Kors of the University of Pennsylvania has noted,

"harassment policies" at a growing number of universities have used the real need to protect students and employees from sexual and racial abuse as a partisan pretext for ... "privileging" one particular ideological agenda, and for controlling speech deemed offensive by those designated as victims of American society (including those "victims" about to receive Ivy League degrees!).

What Professor Kors wrote about the University of Pennsylvania can be applied equally to other institutions intent on mandating virtue for their students and faculty: "In short, Penn is a tolerant and diverse community, and if you do not agree with its particular notions of tolerance and diversity, it will gladly re-educate you." It is little wonder that the president of Yale University, Benno C. Schmidt, should have warned in a recent address that "The most serious problems of freedom of expression in our society today exist on our campuses."

What is going on? The academic elite at most institutions will tell you not to worry, that nothing has happened that need concern parents, trustees, alumni, government or private funding sources. On the issue of enforcing politically correct behavior on campus, for example, they will assure you that the whole thing has been overblown by "conservative" journalists who can't appreciate that the free exchange of ideas must sometimes be curtailed for the higher virtue of protecting the feelings of designated victim groups.

As I have shown in my book *Tenured Radicals*, however, the truth is far more dismaying than the new academic mandarins let on. What we are facing is nothing less than a challenge to the fundamental premises that have traditionally supported both liberal education and a liberal democratic polity. What is at stake? A short list includes respect for rationality and the rights of the individual; a commitment to the ideals of disinterested scholarship and objectivity; freedom of expression; color-blind justice; advancement according to merit, not according to sex, race or ethnic origin. These quintessentially liberal ideas are bedrocks of our political as well as our educational system. And they are precisely the ideas that are now under attack by *bien pensants* academics intoxicated with the thought of their own virtue.

Especially disturbing is the way in which demands for ideological conformity have begun to encroach on basic intellectual freedoms. All those "anti-harassment" policies, ostensibly designed to prevent sexual, ethnic and racial harassment, actually represent a concerted effort to curtail the expression of unpopular ideas and attitudes. Restrictions on what can be said and talked about apply inside as well as outside the classroom, and they have had—in the words of a brief by the Michigan American Civil Liberties Union—a "chilling effect on the free expression of ideas" in the university.

What we are witnessing is a tyrannical combination of extreme license with an almost puritanical censorship. Reflecting on the new demand for intellectual conformity, Donald Kagan, dean of Yale College, notes that he "was a student during the days of McCarthy, and there is less freedom now than there was then." The situation — is it Orwellian or Kafkaesque? — occasionally waxes so bizarre that it seems almost funny. For example, Smith College, in a brochure distributed to incoming students, rehearses a long list of politically incorrect attitudes and prejudices, including the sin of "lookism," i.e., the prejudice of believing that some people are more attractive than others.

It is a strange situation. All indications are that American society as a whole is far more tolerant of diversity now than at any time in the past. Yet in their zeal to nominate themselves as victims of a repressive society, today's academic radicals pretend to find sexism, racism, elitism, "heterosexualism," "lookism" and various other "isms" everywhere. Thus we have Donna Shalala, chancellor of the University of Wisconsin, claiming that "The university is institutionally racist. American society is racist and sexist. Covert racism is just as bad today as overt racism was 30 years ago." In addition to being grossly irresponsible (especially in the mouth of a university chancellor), such unfounded charges of racism, sexism and so on make it all the more difficult to discern or criticize the real thing when it does occur.

The late Sidney Hook got to the heart of the issue when he observed that

> [a]s morally offensive as is the expression of racism wherever it is found, a false charge of racism is equally offensive, perhaps even more so, because the consequences of a false charge of racism enable an authentic racist to conceal his racism by exploiting the loose way the term is used to cover up his actions. The same is true of a false charge of sexism or anti-Semitism. This is the lesson we should all have learned from the days of Senator Joseph McCarthy. Because of his false and irresponsible charges of communism against liberals, socialists, and others among his critics, many communists and agents of communist influence sought to pass themselves off as Jeffersonian democrats or merely idealistic reformers. They would all complain they were victims of red-baiting to prevent criticism and exposure.

It is worth pondering Sidney Hook's remarks as one attempts to digest the unending charges of "isms" pouring forth from the academy today.

Responsible persons will naturally deplore speech and action that hurts the feelings of others. But what does it mean that the university, traditionally a bastion of free speech and a place where controversial ideas could freely circulate, has begun to capitulate to the demand for political orthodoxy? What does it mean, for example, that Barbara Johnson, a well-known professor of French at Harvard University, should declare that "professors should have less freedom of expression than writers and artists, because professors are supposed to be creating a better world"?

Such statements are obnoxious not simply because they betray extraordinary presumption — as if professors had some special purchase on "creating a better world." There is also the basic constitutional issue that such anti-harassment policies violate the right to free speech guaranteed by the First Amendment. But for many academics it would seem that sacrificing the First Amendment is a small price to pay for the display of superior virtue. A leader of the student government at Stanford University in 1989 summed it up this way: "What we are proposing is not completely in line with the First Amendment. But I'm not sure it should be. We at Stanford are trying to set a different standard from what society at large is trying to accomplish." It is a sobering irony that what began as an appeal by the left for "free speech" at Berkeley in the '60s has ended up being an equally fervent appeal by the left for the imposition of censorship.

Indeed, the whole phenomenon of political correctness is rife with ironies. After spending more than two decades attempting to destroy every trace of propriety and mannerly decorum on campus, our tenured or soon-to-be-tenured radicals are now promulgating codes as sweeping as they are vague to regulate speech and expression. Those who 15 minutes ago were telling us that there is no such thing as truth, that all values are relative, that morality is strictly a "personal" matter, are now clamoring for the imposition of stringent controls on speech — all in the name of a higher virtue and sensitivity.

It is important to emphasize too that the new speech codes are not aimed exclusively or even primarily at prohibiting racial slurs or what the law calls "fighting words." Protection from verbal abuse had already — and rightly — been part of the traditional notion of proper behavior. The presumed jurisdiction of the new regulations extends beyond content to the tone and attitude of what is said, written, published and debated. "Misdirected laughter," for example, is routinely regarded as a punishable offense on many campuses. In some cases the new academic thought police even attempt to regulate what is not said, as when an editor of a student newspaper was removed from his post because he had given "insufficient coverage" to minority events.

Far from representing a return to civility, as many academics suggest, the hegemony of political correctness on college campuses today is essentially a campaign of intellectual and moral indoctrination. With its roots in the political agitations of the '60s, the movement for political correctness represents the institutionalization of radicalism. No longer is the threat coming from outside: Now we find professors, deans, provosts and even university presidents militating to recast the traditional, liberal ethos of the academy in the image of multicultural radicalism.

Like most modern tyrannies, the dictatorship of the politically correct freely uses and abuses the rhetoric of virtue in its effort to enforce conformity and silence dissent. This is part of what makes it so seductive. How gratifying to know that one is automatically on the side of Virtue! But the union of moralism and radicalism, while hardly a novel marriage, is particularly destructive in an institution dedicated to intellectual inquiry. Not only does it foster an atmosphere of intimidation and encourage conformity, but it also attacks the very basis for the free exchange of ideas. Anyone concerned about the future of liberal education — indeed, of our liberal, democratic society — has ample grounds for alarm.

Roger Kimball is managing editor of *The New Criterion*, and art critic for the *Wall Street Journal*.

PART V

Book Review

The Academy and Its Discontents

James W. Carey

Illiberal Education: The Politics of Race and Sex on Campus
by Dinesh D'Souza (The Free Press, 1991)

Tenured Radicals: How Politics Has Corrupted Our Higher Education
by Roger Kimball (Harper and Row, 1990)

Killing the Spirit: Higher Education in America
by Page Smith (Viking Penguin, 1990)

ProfScam: Professors and the Demise of Higher Education
by Charles J. Sykes (Regnery Gateway, 1988)

The Hollow Men: Politics and Corruption in Higher Education
by Charles J. Sykes (Regnery Gateway, 1990)

A recent news story in the *New York Times* provides a smallened image of the current crisis in higher education. Lee M. Bass has provided a gift of $20 million to Yale University, bringing to $60 million the gifts provided Yale in recent years by the fabled Bass brothers of Fort Worth, Texas. The current gift is to create "an elective course of studies in Western civilization." The *Times* dutifully puts the gift in its proper political context by noting that Western civilization is "a field that for more than a decade has been under attack while many colleges and universities increased their emphasis on the study of people and cultures outside the Western tradition." The *Times* goes on to note the larger educational significance of the move by Yale: "In the past, strong curriculum moves like this by Yale or other Ivy League institutions have set standards followed by hundreds of other private and public colleges and universities around the country."

The Bass gift was apparently inspired by a speech of Donald Kagan, the dean of Yale College and one of the more thoughtful conservative critics of the modern university. Predictably and disappointingly, the purpose of the Bass largesse was applauded by conservative scholars such as Stephen H. Balch, president of the National Association of

Scholars, though the takeover of the academy by the business elite is an outcome that genuine academic conservatives should greatly fear. Others noted that Yale seemed more interested in acquiring $20 million than in Western civilization. Leon Botstein, the president of Bard College and an advocate of a common intellectual culture for both white and minority students, commented that "To say that Western civilization is important doesn't require $20 million. The question is, why are they saying it? For the donor, for the university, for the public?"

Those are good questions. Yale certainly doesn't require such a large gift in order to place an emphasis on Western culture, if that is what their students most need. The episode has all the appearance of a plutocratic family using its wealth to write the Yale curriculum and a university too uncertain of its purposes, or too weak to act without the justification of an outside gift, to prevent it from doing so.

It is worth mentioning in passing that another of the Bass brothers, Robert, was involved in the attempted takeover of the *St. Petersburg Times*, thereby endangering another educational institution, The Poynter Institute for Media Studies (which I serve as an advisory board member). Robert Bass never announced his educational intentions should he become majority stockholder of the various *Times* companies, but no one was sanguine about the likely outcome. The matter soon became moot, for Robert Bass reduced his role in Florida newspapering, and a new candidate to control the *Times* emerged on the St. Petersburg scene.

A well-known publisher, the same Yale University, investigated its legal claim to ownership of the *St. Petersburg Times*. Yale was a secondary beneficiary of the will of Nelson Poynter, just in case the Poynter Institute was never created, and Yale felt it might have a claim to ownership of the paper, a position it has since abandoned.

All the elements of the mini drama of higher education are here, summarized in Montaigne's lines from "Of Cannibals": "Treachery, disloyalty, cruelty, tyranny, [and to which we might add greed] . . . these are our ordinary vices." The result of such ordinary vice is a volume of criticism aimed at universities that is greater than at any time since the *trahison des clercs* and the plutocratic takeover of the universities in the late stages of industrialism. Killing, corrupting, impoverishing, dying — these are the active and progressive verbs with which the only critics we have at the moment describe what is happening in the citadels of higher learning.

In retrospect, the publication in 1987 of Allan Bloom's *The Closing of the American Mind* was the opening salvo in a concerted campaign to undermine our faith in education. Bloom's book, subtitled "How Higher Education Has Failed Democracy and Impoverished the Souls of Today's Students," set the tone for all that followed and was, curiously enough, fundamentally antidemocratic in spirit and both ignorant and dismissive of youth culture. Bloom's book generated an enormous volume of criticism in the popular media, most of it supportive. However *The Closing of the American Mind* remained virtually undiscussed on the campuses of the country. If universities were as healthy as they often pretend to be, his work would have been subjected to the most rigorous, systematic and evenhanded debate on the campus. In fact, it was largely greeted with dismissive cocktail-party chatter and left entirely outside the established circuits of serious discussion. The trenchant, opposed public reviews were often by figures like Sidney Hook, at whom *The Closing of the American Mind* was not particularly aimed.

Bloom's book deserved serious attention, for it was written by a teacher seriously devoted to education. It was a conservative rather than a right-wing book; it defended a virtue and a value rather than merely promote an interest. And it advanced a number of important arguments, including one apposite to today's circumstances, namely, that the current wave of egalitarianism just may be the reverse side of the individualism that dominates the culture: an individualism through which persons are deracinated, shorn of any tradition or cultural specificity, pretenders to self-created personalities.

Instead of causing serious introspection among faculty and administrators, *The Closing of the American Mind* was simply ignored as if higher education was beyond serious criticism. Unfortunately, much of Bloom's subtle and nuanced criticism was on target, and many of the more recent attacks that have come in its wake are richly deserved. Universities have not been performing very well of late and, like most American institutions, are suffering from a confusion of purposes, an excess of ambition that borders on hubris, and an appetite for money that is truly alarming.

In this century criticism of the American university has characteristically come from the left. Thorstein Veblen's *The Higher Learning in American* and Upton Sinclair's *The Goose-Step* are exemplars from the post-World War I era. Both books savaged the captains of industry and captains of erudition that had seized hold of the universities in the spirit of business enterprise. Today, left-wing criticism of higher education has virtually disappeared even though universities are more than ever run as corporate enterprises and are increasingly dominated by colleges of engineering and business, really Colleges of Capitalism. The books that are the occasion for this review are all written from the political right and by people currently outside the academy. Curiously enough, they have not been answered by the political left, except within the safe confines of sectarian media, nor have they been systematically reviewed by defenders of the academy or much commented on by the university administrators responsible for much of the alleged villainy. As with Bloom's book, university administrators have defensively dismissed all these works without ever really taking account of them. The tenured radicals, who in one fantasy are taking over the universities when they can in truth rarely win the chairmanship of a department, deal with these works by calling a conference of the already committed, exchange pieties agreed upon in advance and otherwise sing praise to their own infallibility. This gives Roger Kimball yet another opportunity to see the left in action (he does his research by showing up at such gatherings) and the left cooperates by staging a show of smug self-satisfaction and dreadful manners that confirms everyone's worst nightmare.

Don't get me wrong: I would not make a case for any of these books with the single exception of D'Souza's *Illiberal Education*, which is a genuine attempt, despite its impeccable conservative credentials, to present a balanced critique of higher education, one that is genuinely sympathetic to the plight of minority students. D'Souza deserves a wide audience and generous and thoughtful consideration even among the academic left. He has a balanced and penetrating view of higher education and, so much the better, writes with an authentically democratic spirit. The other books are less efforts to analyze education than to recruit followers to the right-wing cause or settle old grudges. But, every one of these books, dreadful or not as intellectual work, raises issues that are fateful for higher education and point to serious problems on the campus. It is the general unwillingness to admit to the problems, to tackle them head on, to engage in and widen the debate, that reveals the real weakness of higher education in America. Even intellectually serious work, such as Thomas Sowell's book on what he takes to be the worldwide failure of affirmative action, is greeted with silence or dismissed as conservative or reactionary as if it can be dispensed with by the mere act of labeling.

That silence and that dismissiveness give credence to one charge leveled by all these authors, namely that the conditions of free speech and open debate have evaporated on the campus and have been replaced by timidity and intimidation. For all the hysteria and media hype surrounding "political correctness," there is something to it, as anyone who attends academic gatherings knows. I agree with Yale's Donald Kagan that there is less freedom on the campus now than in the days of Joe McCarthy and, alas, it is narrowing as well far beyond the halls of ivy.

Charles Sykes' *ProfScam* is the most general indictment and analysis of the decline of the quality, pertinence and purpose of higher education. It is a careless and hyperbolic book but often close to the mark in its analysis of the culture of the faculty common rooms. In *The Hollow Men*, his new book, Sykes reveals his true credentials and has benefited from the usual right-wing support, but the book is largely a case study of Dartmouth College and, on the evidence presented, Dartmouth has been in such bad shape for such a long time that it is not so easy to compare it to anything else. The subject common to all the books is the decline of Western civilization, or at least the meaningful study thereof, via the destruction of the traditional canon of great books or the emergence of anti-Western ideologies or both. Most also deal with affirmative action, race relations, free speech, feminism, the race-class-gender mantra, and the ruination of literary criticism and the humanities by relativism, subjectivism and deconstructionism.

The central theme, as given by the title of Roger Kimball's book, is the seizure of the core of the university by 1960s radicals, now tenured apparatchiks. The usual catalog of suspects is here: Duke University, Harvard, Yale, Dartmouth, the universities of Michigan and Wisconsin, Berkeley, and each writer makes the increasingly questionable assumption that what happens in such elite schools trickles down through the system of higher education. Not much here on the state colleges or the community colleges or other such places where most education is, for better or worse, going on: a considerable and damning omission, for we don't know what is trickling down and what might be trickling up. There is considerable redundancy in the books — the same atrocity tales endlessly retold — as if there is a central anecdote bank at some conservative Washington think tank accessible through an 800 — no, make that a 900 — number.

The issues raised by these books are important and, as I noted, deserve rigorous discussion. However I remain unconvinced that the critics from the right or, even more, the more occasional respondent from the left have seized on the fundamental problems, or that they proceed from an adequate analysis of the university as an institution. In fact, I don't even think they have situated the specific matters they address — the canon, political correctness, affirmative action, etc. — in the right context. So here is a very brief catalog — annotated, compressed and hyperbolic — of the underlying changes in the university that provide the deep structure of its surface politics.

The loss of autonomy and independence. The American university has never been an ivory tower, never completely independent of its surrounding society. Very few of them are architecturally walled off from their host communities. Land-grant universities were from the outset campuses without walls dedicated to serving their states. The relationship between the university and the society has always been a tense and uneasy one — moments of accommodation alternating with assertions of autonomy. The core of its activities — teaching and the curriculum — has been the domain of the greatest academic freedom and autonomy, and always the most stoutly defended against outside interference. The independence of the university is now pretty much gone, and where it remains it is largely a pretense.

Perhaps the first breach came with the development of intercollegiate athletics, followed by the seizure of control of boards of trustees by the business community. In the years after World War II, as universities became the research arm of society, the Department of Defense, the various institutes of health, and indeed the entire federal apparatus became a daily and directive presence on the campus. During the 1960s the New Left made a run at expelling the defense establishment, but not in the name of autonomy. It too wanted the university "to be responsive to the community," but to different and presumably more progressive wings of the community. The university did not get rid of the Department of Defense; it just acquired a new set of interest groups with claims on teaching and research. Today boards of trustees increasingly represent the claims of these new groups and are little interested in the welfare of the educational institution as such. When you add to this mix the increasing power of accrediting agencies representing the interests of professional groups, the area of academic autonomy is further diminished. And the alumni. As we saw in the Bass case, the alumni are no longer just giving money to repay *alma mater*; they are increasingly directing what should be built and where, what should be taught and how. For generations now universities have been quietly sold off, piece by piece, to the highest bidder. No one seems to be particularly opposed to this process, though everyone wishes the purchase would be made by an ideological clique with which they are aligned.

The brackish politics and the criticism of the university are played out, then, in a context in which the university has pretty much disappeared as an independent and unitary institution. The university is little more than a balance sheet, but a balance sheet that is the crossroads of the social agenda and the site of interest-group struggles over the next generation of citizens, workers and knowledge.

As the edges of the university become both more porous and indistinct, its internal structure collapses. The only authority left is the authority of money, and that, above all else, is the thing most susceptible to outside control. The real lesson of the 1960s is that when push comes to shove, as it frequently did, the only structure left is a dialectic between the crowd and the police. The university in this sense has become a mass society with no internal structures of authority and decision-making. The only thing standing behind hapless administrators is the coercive power of the state; their only resource the ability to negotiate nonnegotiable demands.

Professionalization. The debate in recent books is exclusively about the liberal arts core of the university. But, in fact, the university has been seized by professional schools and professional education, another mark of their porousness. Despite distribution requirements, most students seek a professional education and, indeed, most of the sound education occurring is found in professional schools. This is because the faculty of professional schools must take real responsibility for their students or be thoroughly disgraced. This is hardly true in the old liberal arts, where faculty do not have and do not want a relationship with students in which they are publicly responsible for what students learn and what they become. This is true even at Ivy League schools. In my most recent perusal, the largest undergraduate major at Harvard was economics, and that is so not because students have fallen into a swoon with the subject matter, but because economics is the closest thing a student can get to a professional education in Cambridge in the absence of an undergraduate business school.

The liberal arts have become professionalized also because those disciplines are driven by doctoral programs, and the curriculum increasingly reflects not the needs of students but the research needs and professional interests of faculty. Professionalization, then, has a double edge: the spread of education in the professions throughout undergraduate school, and the professionalization of the liberal arts as those disciplines increasingly reflect the professional interests and status of the faculty. The curriculum is further professionalized, often silently, by the spread of the internship system, which in liberal arts colleges is another way students can acquire a professional education without it showing up on the university transcript. Internships, in which work is traded for money, for so-called "real world" experience, eat up increasing amounts of student credit hours. For the university it is cheap and invisible training that allows students to feel they are being prepared for an occupation, but it also turns education over to business firms, interests groups and professional societies. (I am stunned that conservatives neither noticed nor protested against the degree to which the campaign against the nomination of Robert Bork to the Supreme Court was fueled by the availability of student interns all over Washington. The interns did the free or cheap work necessary to create the "book of Bork" and to otherwise execute the thousands of tasks necessary to mount a judicial plebiscite. The lesson: never nominate anyone for the court on July 1. For details see Michael Pertschuk's *The People Rising*. Unfortunately, the use of interns is not confined to left-wing organizations; the right does not object to unpaid labor either.)

The central point is this. With the spread of professional education through undergraduate life and the professional spirit throughout all education, the central issue, to steal and paraphrase some lines from Ernest J. Weinrib, is whether education is to be understood in instrumental or noninstrumental terms. Professional education is necessarily instrumental and inevitably, to some degree, ideological. But only insofar as the education at the core of university life is conceived as non-instrumental can education be insulated from the purposes which political and economic interests wish to project onto it. At stake is a conceptual point about education, not an empirical one, about the degree to which any given educational system realizes in practice education of a noninstrumental nature. The dismissal of education as necessarily ideological implies not only that education is an instrument available for exploitation by hierarchically entrenched groups, but that it can be nothing else. It denies the possibility that there can be any noninstrumental understanding of any form of pedagogy, and it is the point of agreement between the left and the right, between most of the current critics of the academy and, in a phrase of Henry Gates, "the rainbow coalition of feminists, deconstructionists, Althusserians, Foucauldians, people working in ethnic and gay studies" whom they criticize. For both these groups all education is necessarily and desirably instrumental and ideological: Education always represents an interest rather than pursues a virtue. It all comes down to whose ox gets gored.

The spread of student services. During the 1960s the doctrine of *in loco parentis* was pretty much thrown out every place. This left the student-services wing of the campus, what we used to call the dean of students office, without much to do except paper and custodial work. Unemployment is not accepted easily anywhere, and, therefore, student services had to find a new basis for its work and authority. In parallel with the culture as a whole, the new justification was found in the medicalization of the student body. Every student problem is now turned into an occasion for therapy and a course, frequently an academic one, analyzing the cause, symptoms and cure not only of traditional student ailments but of a legion of newly invented problems. Naturally, in the era of racism, sexism, homophobia and multiculturalism, student services is having a field day. Financed through student fees (largely outside of tuition and tax money), student services has had opportunities to grow faster and more rapaciously than the academic wing of the university. This growth is further impelled and justified by the more traditional doctrine that "the major part of the student's education occurs outside the classroom," even if it is education in the self-recognition of symptoms.

Student services, then, has been one of the sites of the principal force in the erosion of education, namely credit inflation. (Yes, universities also give internship credit for unpaid, nonacademic work, thus rewarding students for doing some of the busy work of administration.) It is impossible to estimate the actual worth and content of the old 124-credit-hour graduation requirement, but I would guess that it is worth about 80 hours these days. Credit inflation has occurred by converting the extra-curricular into the curricula, thereby giving credit for what was once leisure, club work or medical therapy. In addition, courses that were once, say, worth three hours are raised to four credit hours without a corresponding change in either the amount or difficulty of the work involved. Student services has plenty of coconspirators in this because the dilution of the curriculum through inflation has certain decided advantages for the faculty: fewer hours of less intense teaching, more hours taught by outside firms and groups and by nonfaculty, more advising turned over to nonacademic staff. The consequence is the active devaluing and dilution of the academic curriculum, which in turn has created more problems with which student services has to deal. For example, a major part of the "alcohol problem on campus" comes from the active revaluing of leisure as educational and the structuring of courses and curricula so that Friday becomes a classless day and the drinking weekend begins on Thursday night. The real losers in all this are the students, and particularly those newest and least prepared for higher education. It gives credence to the question James Baldwin asked in the 1960s in *The Fire Next Time*: "Do I want to be integrated into a burning house?"

These, then, are but a few of the underlying problems and forces in higher education that escape the critics and provide the real setting in which the surface political struggles are played out. The loss of autonomy, the absolute penetration of the university by the haphazard forces of the social, the dissolution of a structure of legitimate governance and authority, the medicalization of students, the professionalization and instrumentalization of the curriculum that turn it into an ideological battle ground, the inflation of credit and devaluation of academic study: These are the problems that will have to be solved before any meaningful attempt can be made to debate Western civilization, affirmative action, political correctness or any of the other issues, as important as they are, that critics scrape off the political surface of university life.

There is a subject I have not treated that is of decisive importance in assessing universities, namely a careful examination of the relative state of various disciplines. I have emphasized matters that are extrinsic to the disciplines, but there is much to be said about the intrinsic conditions of various parts of the university's curriculum. For example, despite the lead taken by hard scientists in breaching the walls of the academy, in developing an all too cozy relation to the state and industry, the physical sciences are largely sites of real achievement and great vitality. The major problems are in the "softer" disciplines, the humanities and social sciences. Despite my hopes for the humanities, large parts of the relevant disciplines are scenes of moral collapse and the posturing of the privileged: conduct that has cost them their authority and, if the truth be known, their self-confidence. And, despite the fact it is the social sciences from which I began my particular journey, those sciences are frequently as barren as a desert and as inhospitable to life as a moonscape; they are now ruled by a form of social engineering that appeals to the utopian longings of the deracinated.

The debate between the left and the right, the neoconservatives and the rainbow coalition, is one in which we, those seriously concerned about universities and higher education, ought not to take part. It is a debate in which the antagonists despise their opponents too much even to argue with them. It is, in fact, no debate at all, and we shall have to work orthogonally to the established lines of argument.

The Czech writer Milan Kundera has said that the best novels do not merely confirm what we already know but uncover new aspects of existence. The same can be said for the best criticism. It never merely adds decibels to one side or another of an existing argument, never merely engages in verbal gunfire from a fixed position. The books reviewed here are, with the single exception of D'Souza's *Illiberal Education*, inadequate and unhelpful criticism. They give truth to the acid comment of Alsadair MacIntyre that modern politics cannot be a matter of moral consensus; it is a civil war carried on by other means. But again, it is a war into which we ought not to allow ourselves to be drawn, for any substantial change in education, never mind our more general politics, is going to require a new coalition of people drawn from across the political spectrum who revolt against the uncivil lines and habits of argument that are at the moment destroying the possibilities of public life and with them the people, generally minorities and the underclass, who would benefit most from a less ideological, more pragmatic and generally more civil form of discourse.

For example, I cannot under present circumstances imagine a principled argument for or against black studies or women's studies or affirmative action. It all depends. Black studies and women's studies have already registered real scholarly achievements, and under the right circumstances promise much more of value to students and the general culture. They arose not solely for political reasons but for scholarly ones as well. Important subjects and issues could not work themselves onto the scholarly agenda; they were frozen out of intellectual discourse, scholarly research and systematic teaching because of the existing distributions of disciplinary interest. As someone who spent much of his early career trying to clear some space in the university for the study of the mass media and for its legitimate institutionalization, I know something of what faculty in black and women's studies are up against.

At any given moment the distribution of disciplinary interest may bear little relation to the importance of problems, the needs of students or the interests of faculty new to the university. Already some of the most interesting work on a range of critical problems is occurring in these new disciplines. And, naturally, it is now spreading backward into established departments just as today the study of mass communication can be found in many traditional places in the university. It just took a while for others to catch on. And woe to those new departments when the traditional disciplines finally do catch on. (The catching-on process, incidentally, is slower to the precise degree that the subject matter is unorthodox or emerges from the less advantaged segments of the population. A few decades of the study of culture has at least taught us that.) Of course, black and women's studies could end up very badly; there are no guarantees. And they *will* turn out badly if they are treated with scorn, exempted from the most rigorous academic standards out of misplaced and condescending sympathy, or completely politicized and used as an excuse to balkanize the university.

The same type of argument should be made about affirmative action. The purpose of such programs is to expand the pool of society's talent by drawing into the academy those from disadvantaged classes who have the most to contribute to education and the professions. Discrimination injures the social order not only by keeping some talented people out, but by protecting the unqualified who got in only because others were denied access. As an affirmative action admit of another generation, before the process had a name, one admitted not on the basis of race but class and disability, I have a real investment in the legitimacy of this process and a real sympathy for those today being unfairly stigmatized and victimized by it. Affirmative action will fail also if it becomes largely a cover for an undisclosed political purpose, if large numbers of minorities are placed in situations that guarantee failure, if it is used by the comfortable middle class to discriminate against others stigmatized as being white or Asian, if, in short, its purposes are subverted by the antidemocratic and anti-egalitarian tendencies of those who, because they have no children or do not care about children or can guarantee their children a place in the occupational and cultural hierarchy, can treat a noble attempt with complete cynicism.

The conclusion is inescapable that the existing partners in this debate, with some notable exceptions, have given up all hope for democracy and education however much they invoke both. The evidence for this is in the treatment accorded E.D. Hirsch Jr.'s *Cultural Literacy*, which encounters scorn and dismissal from both groups. Hirsch proposes a rather simple and I should think uncontroversial idea: If members of the same political society, those age 16 and those age 60, those in the same town and those separated by thousands of miles, are going to talk meaningfully to one another it helps a great deal if they share something of a common culture.

At the simplest level a common culture consists of a lot of proper nouns referring to persons, events, objects, places, dates, etc. that facilitate mutual understanding. The schools have been doing a rather bad job of transmitting even this simplest form of culture, so Hirsch has taken the risks of working with school systems and developing lists of what it is Americans should know in common. The proposed lists, which are clearly hypothetical and experimental, are as odd and assorted as one might expect in a large, heterogeneous country divided by race, ethnicity and religion. The lists also draw items from all "class levels" in recognition of the breakdown of the old distinctions between high, popular, folk and mass culture. For this Hirsch is regularly dismissed and pilloried as the purveyor of trivial pursuits and attacked as the common enemy of both the left and the right, an attack that only reveals the hostility against a common culture not constructed on an explicit ideological agenda.

A common culture for conversation and communication of the least ideological kind is feared by the politically committed because of the forms of social relations such a culture would permit. When I was growing up in Rhode Island, for example, we were taught among other things who Roger Williams was. The teachers thought it would help us identify Roger Williams Hospital and Roger Williams Park. We might also learn something along the way about the tradition of religious liberty Williams founded in the state when he fled Massachusetts. We were also taught the names of the towns in the state and where they came from, and something of the rivers and lakes and other identifiable features of the landscape. One cannot dignify this as geography or history or social science, but it surely is useful if you wish to hold an intelligible conversation or write a letter to the editor.

But the response to Hirsch raises again the question of who is interested in education. The right and the left seem to have little interest in it or in a common culture or much else. Their relation to students is a purely instrumental one: recruits to one political cause or another, recruits to one occupational cadre or another. Students are rarely seen as potential citizens and neighbors capable of making independent contributions to a common life. Both groups lack an embracing sense of citizenship and seem most driven by the urge, all appearances to the contrary, to deracinate the student body as the precondition of producing docile followers of a political ideology or docile consumers of the gross national product. At the root of the discussion of the canon and other issues in higher education is a vulgar notion of culture and human potential. Few of the critics, left or right, have read or, if read, absorbed the best that has been thought and written on the subject of the canon and culture, such as the work of Raymond Williams and Eugene Goodheart. What are we, after all, to make of this, and what, after all, are we to do about it?

I do know, at least, the major temptation we will have to resist. In recent years universities have fallen in love with publicity and devote much energy to arranging and manipulating it. They forgot that Lewis Mumford included publicity, along with political power, productivity, profit and power, as part of the Pentagon of Power: the syndrome of forces that universities had to avoid if they were to preserve a love of learning. Universities are now reaping the consequences of their willingness to play the publicity game, for the media are turning against them. The recent works on higher education are, Dinesh D'Souza again excepted, part of a publicity contest, part of, as I said at the outset, a sustained attempt to undermine our capacity to have faith in higher education. They are pitched as media products, entries into the game of publicity. Predictably, we will soon have a counterattack from the universities: more media products designed to exploit faith and credibility. It is a contest that higher education will lose, indeed will deserve to lose.

It is not that there is a gulf between higher education and the media, a separation created by mutual arrogance, though there is plenty of arrogance to go around. The media always move back and forth across the center line of politics in concert with perceived shifts in public sentiment. They have now drifted to the right and happily join the campaign to expose the failures and follies of the academy. One cannot count on the media to join and illuminate the debate on higher education, but rather to orchestrate the publicity toward one political tendency or another, currently toward the right. Those of us who care about education and are marooned at the moment need whatever help we can get and from whatever quarter we can get it. Meanwhile, as my friend Stuart Adam says, we in universities "are surrounded by bureaucrats. Where are the poets?"

James W. Carey was dean of the College of Communications at the University of Illinois until 1992, and subsequently a visiting professor at the Graduate School of Journalism, Columbia University.

Index

ABC News, 53
Academia: critics of, xiii–xiv, 16, 30–31, 154–66; educational and communicative role of, 2, 10–11, 62–63, 67–72; as ivory tower, 22–23, 158; major issues facing, 6–10; politicization of, 7–10, 137–50, 157; relations with media, xv, 5–10, 45–52, 61–65, 109–11, 166–67; similarities to media, 5–6, 109–11. *See also* Colleges and universities; Education reporting
Academic freedom, xii, 5–6, 23, 141–43. *See also* Freedom of speech
Active (practice) scholarship, 126–31
Adam, Stuart, 167
Addison-Wesley, 129, 130
Affirmative action, 163–65
Ajami, Fouad, 53–54, 57–58
Alumni, 16, 50, 159
Alumni magazines, 88–96
American Collegiate Network, 97
American Higher Education: 1958 (report), 89
Annenberg School of Communications, 100
Apollo Computer, 116
Apple Computer, 116, 131
Arkansas, 78
Associated Collegiate Press' National Pacemaker Award, 100
Association of Research Libraries (ARL), 128, 131
Atchley, William, 83
Athletes, graduation rate, 73–74
Athletic departments: financial health of, 77–79, 82; fraud and misconduct of, 79–83; media propaganda for, 74–76
Athletics. *See* College sports

Balakian, Nona, 93
Balch, Stephen, 153–54
Baldwin, James, 106, 162
Bantam Books, 93
Bass, Lee M., 153

Bass, Robert, 154
Batke, Peter, 128–29
Bennett, William, xiii, 7–8
Berry, Wendell, 110
Bethell, John, 91–94
BITNET, 123
Black studies, 163–64
Bliwise, Robert L., 93
Bloom, Allan, 139; *The Closing of the American Mind*, xiii, 155
Bloomington (Indiana) Herald-Times, 74–75
Bok, Derek, xii, 35
Bookshelf (CD-ROM database), 130
Bork, Robert, 143, 160
Boston Globe, 57–58
Boston University, 140–43
Bostonia, 93
Botstein, Leon, 154
Boyer, Ernest, xiii
Brecht, Bertolt, 143
Brokaw, Tom, 53
Bromley, Allen, 8
Brown, Donald, 127
Brown Alumni Monthly, 89, 115
Brown University, computerization project, 115–23
BRUNET (Brown University), 117
BRUNO (Brown University), 122
Brzezinski, Zbigniew, 57
Bulliet, Richard, 57
Bush, George, 131, 143
Business. *See* Corporate sector
Butler, Nicholas Murray, 109

California Institute of Technology, 36
Canada, 23, 25–28
Carnegie Corporation, 89
Carnegie Mellon University, 47
Carroll, Admiral Eugene, 54
Carter, Barry, 55, 57
Carter, Hodding, III, 55, 71
Catalog, on-line, 119–20
CAUSE, 128, 131